100
ways
with
eggs

100
ways
with
eggs

boiled, baked, fried, scrambled & more!

RYLAND PETERS & SMALL
LONDON • NEW YORK

Designer Barbara Zúñiga
Picture Manager Christina Borsi
Commissioning Editor Stephanie Milner
Head of Production Patricia Harrington
Art Director Leslie Harrington
Editorial Director Julia Charles
Publisher Cindy Richards

Indexer Hilary Bird

First published in 2016 by
Ryland Peters & Small
20–21 Jockey's Fields,
London WC1R 4BW
and
341 E 116th St,
New York NY 10029
www.rylandpeters.com

10 9 8 7 6 5 4 3 2 1

Recipe collection compiled by Stephanie Milner
Text copyright © Valerie Aikman-Smith, Miranda Ballard,
Ghillie Başan, Fiona Beckett, Vatcharin Bhumichitr, Jordan
Bourke, Maxine Clark, Linda Collister, Ross Dobson, Tori
Finch, Ben Fordham and Felipe Fuentes Cruz, Tonia George,
Tori Haschka, Carol Hilker, Rachael Anne Hill, Jennifer Joyce,
Jenny Linford, Claire and Lucy McDonald, Jane Mason, Dan
May, Hannah Miles, Miisa Mink, Louise Pickford, Isidora
Popovic, Ben Reed, Shelagh Ryan, Laura Santtini, Milli
Taylor, Will Torrent, Fran Warde, Laura Washburn, William
Yeoward and Ryland Peters & Small 2016

Design and photographs copyright © Ryland Peters & Small
2016

For full recipe and photography credits, see page 160.

ISBN: 978-1-84975-773-7

Printed in China

A CIP record for this book is available from the British
Library. US Library of Congress Cataloging-in-Publication
data has been applied for.

notes

- Both British (Metric) and American (Imperial plus
  US cups) measurements are included in these recipes
  for your convenience, however it is important to work
  with one set of measurements and not alternate between
  the two within a recipe.
- All spoon measurements are level unless otherwise
  specified.
- All eggs are medium (UK) or large (US), unless specified
  as large, in which case US extra-large should be used.
  Uncooked or partially cooked eggs should not be served
  to the very old, frail, young children, pregnant women
  or those with compromised immune systems.
- Ovens should be preheated to the specified
  temperatures. We recommend using an oven
  thermometer. If using a fan-assisted oven, adjust
  temperatures according to the manufacturer's
  instructions.
- Whenever butter is called for within these recipes,
  unsalted butter should be used.
- When a recipe calls for the grated zest of citrus fruit,
  buy unwaxed fruit and wash well before using. If you
  can only find treated fruit, scrub well in warm soapy
  water before using.

food safety notice

The information contained within this book is intended as
a general guide to cooking with eggs at home based on the
authors' recipe development and experience. Although all
reasonable care has been taken in the preparation of this
book, neither the publishers nor the authors can accept any
liability for any consequence from the use thereof, or the
information contained therein. Please consult an up-to-date
government source on food safety for further information.

contents

introduction

Eggs, eggs, eggs, eggs, eggs. There are hundreds of ways to prepare, cook with, bake with and even drink eggs, and in this collection of 100 ways with eggs you'll transform a simple scramble into something spectacular, use hard- and soft-boiled/cooked eggs in unusual ways, poach, fry, bake, coddle and much, much more.

Eggs form a nutritious part of our daily diet, whether as the mainstay of breakfasts, in salads, boiled and chopped and as mayonnaise dressings, atop soups or as hot lunches like quiches and frittatas. They can be baked for dinner or transformed into an array of sweet treats, such as meringues, soufflés, cakes and custards. With the rise in popularity of high-protein diets and the irresistible ooze of just-cooked egg yolk, there's no doubt about it; we love eggs!

Both the white and yolk of an egg are rich in nutrients. They are a very good source of inexpensive, high-quality protein. The whites are rich sources of selenium, vitamins D, B6, B12 and minerals such as zinc, iron and copper. Egg yolks contain more calories and fat. They are the source of cholesterol, vitamins A, D, E and K, and lecithin – the compound that enables emulsification in recipes such as Hollandaise sauce (see page 16) or mayonnaise (see page 124). Some brands of egg now contain higher levels of Omega-3 fatty acids, depending on what the hens have been fed. And more than that, eggs are regarded a 'complete' source of protein as they contain all eight essential amino acids.

This recipe collection begins with an introduction to the types of eggs you can buy – from the hen's egg to quail, duck, pheasant and even the extra-large ostrich egg – and how to store them, followed by step-by-step instructions for preparing eggs in a variety of ways. You'll learn to boil, poach, fry, scramble and coddle eggs here, as well as add a few essential skills (for separating and whisking yolks and whites) to your cook's repertoire – keep a look out for the 'cook's notes' on recipe pages for hints and tips on preparation and ingredients.

Once you've mastered these Eggsentials on pages 8–11, the recipes are then organized by type of dish to be enjoyed throughout the day. There are some dishes that everyone should master. From Eggs Benedict (see page 16) to Spanish Omelette (see page 38) and Frittata Bites (see page 99) to soufflés (see pages 119 and 142), you'll make egg-cellent progress with these simple recipes. And for the more adventurous cook, there are ideas for adding fried eggs to Korean Bibimbap (see page 111), poached eggs to Spicy Kimchi Hash Browns (see page 66), scrambling up a Turkish Menemen (see page 65) and whipping up tart fillings with Quiche Lorraine (see page 120) and mini tartlets (see page 104). And finally, things really get interesting with a few classic egg-white cocktails, such as the Whiskey Sour (see page 157), thrown in for good measure.

You'll feel spoilt for choice with this egg-clectic collection of recipes that truly make the most of the humble egg. Get cracking!

eggsentials

There are a wide variety of eggs available in supermarkets, whole food stores, farmers' markets and even through local hen-keepers. Different birds produce different eggs that each have distinctive features; some are bigger than others and some have brighter coloured yolks or richer flavour. Many of the recipes in this book could make use of a variety of eggs, so get to know what's what here then experiment as you go along. It's an egg-citing adventure!

hen's eggs

Available in different colours and sizes, the most common hen's eggs in supermarkets are UK medium/US large in brown and white shells. The colour of the shell is dictated by the kind of hen that produces the egg. Free-range eggs come from hens that live in barns or on farms and have a set amount of time spent outside each day. Certified organic eggs come from hens that enjoy more access to the outdoors than free-range birds, less crowded living conditions and an organic diet.

Hen's eggs are often available as 'Omega-3 rich' where the hen's diet has been naturally enriched with Omega-3 fatty acids as a good way for consumers to boost their Omega-3 intake. Other specialist hen's eggs, such as Clarence Court® Burford Browns and Costwold Legbars, are available from heritage breed hens that are renowned for their flavour, larger yolks, firmer whites and stronger shells. These are widely available in the UK, but specialist heritage breed eggs can also be sourced worldwide from farmers' markets and are well worth trying at home.

quail eggs

Miniature eggs from the diminutive quail are about the same size as a large olive, making them the perfect size for creating appetizers like the Scotch eggs on pages 87 and 91. With speckled brown shells, they have a higher proportion of yolk to white than hen's eggs but can be prepared in the same way for shorter periods of cooking time, reflecting their smaller size.

cook's note: *quail eggs can be fiddly to shell affter boiling so allow a little extra time for this task if replacing hen's eggs with quail's when following the recipes for boiled eggs in this book.*

pheasant eggs

Larger than quail's eggs but around half the size of hen's eggs, pheasant eggs have a deep yellow yolk and come in olive-green or brown shells.

duck eggs

Duck eggs are a luxurious alternative to hen's eggs and come in white or pale blue shells. Much bigger with a richer yolk and a higher concentration of

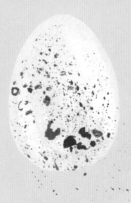

nutrients, specifically protein, they can be excellent additions to salads such as the Salad Kaek and Potato Salad on page 124. You can cook duck eggs in the same way you would cook any other eggs but because of their higher fat content, they won't always make a good substitute in baking, when recipes will need a little trial and testing to perfect. They are however very popular in Asian dishes because of their strong flavour, so try out the Mee Grob on page 135 using a duck egg for something a little different.

turkey eggs

Much creamier than hen's eggs, turkey eggs have a very high ratio of yolk to white. In speckled shells, they are delicious fried, poached or boiled (methods that show off the yolk).

goose eggs

Rich and creamy, these white-shelled eggs are roughly the equivalent of two hen's eggs – the perfect size for an omelette, soft-boiling/cooking and dipping into or even scrambling.

ostrich eggs

The super-sized ostrich egg is equivalent to roughly 24 hen's eggs. While similar in taste and texture to the hen's egg, this enormous variety can taste a little gamey and is not as readily available in supermarkets.

egg whites

Liquid egg whites are available in bottles or cartons in most supermarkets and are ideal for whipping up meringues or egg white omelettes without having to worry about what to do with the leftover yolks.

storing eggs

Store eggs in their box in the fridge or below 20°C (68°F) to maintain freshness. Keep them pointed-end down and away from strong-smelling foods, as they are extremely porous and can absorb odours through their shells. Use by the 'best-before' date. To test for freshness, fill a large mixing bowl with water – a fresh egg will sink in water; a stale one will float and should be discarded.

safety tip: *Wash hands before and after handling eggs, and discard any cracked and/or dirty eggs.*

For many recipes, including cakes and pastry, eggs should be at room temperature. Take them out of the fridge 30 minutes–1 hour before using. To bring cold eggs to room temperature more quickly, immerse them in a bowl of warm (not hot) water for a few minutes. Cold eggs may crack when you boil them in the shell and egg whites at room temperature will whisk better than cold egg whites.

Freeze egg yolks, first mixing them with a little salt or sugar (½–1 teaspoon per two yolks), in a covered plastic container for up to 3 months. Freeze egg whites in a covered plastic container for up to 6 months. Remember to include the number of yolks or whites, and whether they are sweet or salted, on the label. Once thawed, use on the same day and do not refreeze.

how to crack an egg

There are two ways to crack eggs. Either hold an egg in one hand and carefully use a table knife to crack the egg in the middle. Put your thumbs into the crack and pull the eggshell apart. Let the egg fall into a bowl. Fish out any broken eggshell using a larger piece of eggshell that will attract the smaller piece to it through the egg rather than chasing the shell around with a spoon. Or, if you prefer, you can crack an egg by bashing it on the side of a bowl, but you might end up with some of the egg dripping down the side of the bowl until you've had a chance to practice! Always wash your hands well after cracking eggs, as it is very easy to pass bacteria from raw food like eggs to cooked food.

how to separate eggs

Crack the egg as above and before pulling it apart, let the yolk settle in one half of the shell. Allow the yolk to rest in one of the open halves, then transfer to the other half, back and forth, dropping the white into the bowl beneath. Tip the yolk into a separate bowl and continue with as many of the eggs as the recipe calls for.

how to boil an egg

Bring a large pan of water to a boil and, when the water is very bubbly, add the eggs and boil for the specified cooking time below. Remove the eggs from the water with a slotted spoon and put in a large bowl filled with ice cubes and water. Serve in egg cups or, when the eggs are cold, tap gently on the side of the bowl and peel.

type of egg	soft-boil/cook	hard-boil/cook
Hen	5–6 minutes	9–10 minutes
Quail	30 seconds	1 minute
Pheasant	2 minutes	3–4 minutes
Duck	4–5 minutes	9–10 minutes
Turkey	5–6 minutes	10–11 minutes
Goose	9–10 minutes	13 minutes
Ostrich	50 minutes	1½–2 hours

how to poach an egg

Crack the egg into a small bowl. Fill a medium frying pan/skillet three-quarters of the way up with water. Add 1 tablespoon of vinegar and set over medium heat until bubbles start to form in the bottom of the pan. Carefully pour the egg (one at a time if poaching more than one) into the water making sure they are well spaced apart. Cook for 4 minutes, then remove with a slotted spoon and drain on paper towels.

Alternatively, fill a deep saucepan with water and bring to the boil over high heat. Reduce the heat to low so the water is barely simmering and break the egg (or eggs far apart if poaching more than one), into the pan. Cook for 3 minutes, then remove with a slotted spoon and drain on paper towels.

how to fry an egg

Add enough oil to a frying pan/skillet to coat the base and set over high heat until the oil glistens. Crack in the eggs and turn the heat to low. Cook for the specified cooking time below, then remove from the pan with a fish slice.

sunny-side up Cook for 2 minutes, then carefully baste the yolk with hot oil to ensure the white is cooked but the yolk is runny

over easy Cook for 2 minutes, then flip over for 30 seconds to cook on the other side but leave the yolk with a bit of ooze

over hard Cook for 2 minutes, then flip over for 1 minute to cook the yolk completely

cook's note: *If you like fried eggs to look neat on the plate, break each one into a greased, round metal cookie cutter in the frying pan/skillet. Alternatively, use a cookie cutter to trim the whites of fried eggs neatly before serving.*

how to scramble an egg

Put a knob/pat of butter in a saucepan. Melt over medium (not high) heat. Add the eggs and cook, stirring with a spoon. Keep stirring to break up the egg. When the eggs are almost cooked – so they look only slightly wet – take the pan off the heat and rest it on a pan stand. Keep stirring until the eggs are cooked – the heat from the pan will continue to cook them.

how to coddle an egg

Line the bottom of a large pan with a clean kitchen cloth and grease the insides of the coddler(s) with butter. Fill the pan with enough water to come up just beneath the rim of the coddler(s) and bring to a boil.

Put ½ teaspoon double/heavy cream into each coddler, add 1 egg and season with salt and pepper. Screw the lids on tightly then carefully place the coddlers into the boiling water.

Reduce the heat and simmer for 3–4 minutes. Remove the pan from the heat and set aside for 6–7 minutes to finish the cooking process.

Remove the coddlers from the water, pat dry, unscrew the lids and serve. You should have a just-cooked, slightly creamy egg to dip into.

whisking egg whites

When whisking egg whites, always start with clean, dry, grease-free equipment. Grease, oil or water in bowls or on whisks will prevent the whites from whisking stiffly. Plastic bowls are not recommended, as the surface is difficult to clean completely of oil or grease; use a stainless steel or glass bowl. Make sure the whites contain no traces of shell or yolks, which contain fat. If a little yolk has fallen into your egg whites, scoop it out, or touch the yolk with a piece of damp paper towel – the yolk should stick to the paper. For best results, use very fresh eggs and add a pinch of salt or cream of tartar at the start to help stiffen them.

cook's note: *Slightly older eggs are better for meringues. They're also easier to separate.*

breakfast & brunch

Scrambled eggs need to be cooked with patience to become creamy. If they are cooked properly, you will not have to resort to adding cream, which just hides an underlying bad scramble. Smoked trout goes exceedingly well with scrambled eggs and the pretty purple leaves of shiso cress add a fiery kick. Research shows that eating oily fish, such as Omega-rich salmon, trout, mackerel and sardines, three times a week, can improve your heart's health! So tuck in and feel free to replace the trout or salmon used here with a hot smoked kipper or grilled peppered mackerel, if you fancy a change.

scrambled eggs with smoked trout & shiso

10 large eggs
4 tablespoons whole milk
50 g/3½ tablespoons butter
4 slices white bread
280 g/10 oz. hot smoked trout, flaked
a handful of shiso cress
a pinch of chilli powder
sea salt and black pepper, to season

scrambled eggs with smoked salmon (optional)
4 tablespoons chopped fresh flat-leaf parsley or snipped chives
4 slices wholemeal/ whole-wheat bread, toasted
180 g/6 oz. sliced smoked salmon
lemon wedges, to serve

serves †

Break the eggs into a mixing bowl and beat together with the milk and some salt and pepper.

Meanwhile, heat half of the butter in a heavy-bottomed saucepan over low heat until the bubbling subsides. Pour in the eggs and heat through, stirring occasionally, for 4–5 minutes, until they start to feel like they are in danger of catching on the base of the pan. Reduce the heat to its lowest setting and stir constantly for 3–5 minutes to make sure the eggs are not over-heating on the bottom of the pan.

Meanwhile, toast and butter the bread with the remaining butter. Take the eggs off the heat while they still look a little runny, add the trout, give them a final few stirs and divide between the pieces of toast. Scatter the shiso cress and a little chilli powder over the top, then serve.

scrambled eggs with smoked salmon

Beat the egg, milk, half the parsley or chives and a little salt and pepper together, and cook as above. Alternatively, pour the mixture into a microwaveable bowl and microwave on the highest setting for 2 minutes, stirring halfway through.

Spoon the scrambled egg onto the toast. Top with the smoked salmon and sprinkle with the remaining parsley or chives. Serve immediately with a wedge of lemon to squeeze over.

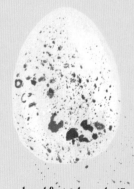

This dish is all about timing. Get everything ready before you cook the eggs and you won't have to rush. Hollandaise sauce made in a blender is easy – add the butter very slowly and you should hear the sauce turning thick and slushy. Substitute the wholemeal/whole-wheat muffin with homemade gluten-free muffins following the recipe below, if desired.

eggs Benedict

4 large eggs
4 wholemeal/whole-
  wheat muffins, halved
  horizontally
8 slices thin-cut ham
black pepper, to season

Hollandaise sauce
2 tablespoons white wine
  vinegar
1 shallot, roughly
  chopped
½ teaspoon black
  peppercorns
2 large egg yolks
120 g/1 stick butter

gluten-free English
muffins (optional)
150 ml/⅔ cup warm milk
1 tablespoon fast-action
  dried yeast
1 tablespoon caster/
  granulated sugar
300 g/2⅓ cups gluten-free
  strong white bread flour
1 teaspoon baking
  powder
1 teaspoon xanthan gum
1 teaspoon salt
1 egg, beaten
80 ml/⅓ cup plain yogurt
60 g/4 tablespoons butter,
  melted and cooled
yellow cornmeal and
  polenta, for dusting

serves 4 and makes
6 muffins

Preheat the grill/broiler to medium.

To make the Hollandaise sauce, put the vinegar, 2 tablespoons of cold water, the shallot and peppercorns in a saucepan and simmer over low heat for a few minutes until you have 1 tablespoon liquid remaining. Strain into a blender (or in a bowl if you are going to use an electric handheld whisk) with the egg yolks and set aside. Melt the butter in the same pan.

Fill a deep frying pan/skillet with water and bring to a demure simmer. Crack the eggs in so they don't touch and poach for exactly 3 minutes.

Put the muffins (cut-side up) and ham on a baking sheet and grill/broil for 2–3 minutes.

To finish the sauce, blend the egg mixture until frothy. With the motor running, add the melted butter in a very slow trickle until the sauce is thick. It should take about a minute to add all the butter; any quicker and it will not emulsify and you'll just have runny eggs.

Drape a slice of ham on top of each muffin half. Scoop out each poached egg and add to the stack. Pour over the Hollandaise sauce and sprinkle with black pepper to serve.

gluten-free English muffins

Put the warm milk, yeast and sugar in a jug/pitcher and leave in a warm place for about 10 minutes until a thick foam has formed on top of the liquid.

Sift the flour, baking powder and xanthan gum into a large mixing bowl. Add the salt, beaten egg, yogurt and melted butter, and mix well with a wooden spoon until everything is incorporated and you have a soft dough. Divide the dough into 6 portions.

Roll each portion into a ball on a surface dusted with the yellow cornmeal. Flatten the balls into patties with straight sides about 3 cm/1 inch high. Sprinkle with polenta and pat down so that it sticks to the dough. Arrange them on a flour-dusted baking sheet and leave uncovered in a warm place for 45–60 minutes.

When the muffins have risen, heat a grill pan over high heat. Grease the pan with a little butter, add the muffins and turn down the heat. Cook for 8–10 minutes on one side, turn over and cook the underneath for a further 7–10 minutes until golden brown and springy to the touch.

This is another lovely brunch option. An open sandwich leaves a little wiggle room for individual tastebuds, so your companions can make up their own forkfuls, adding seasoning to taste.

chorizo, avocado & poached egg open sandwich

4 eggs
4 x 5-cm/2-inch lengths of chorizo sticks, cut in half lengthways
olive oil, to drizzle (or butter, to spread, if preferred)
4 slices soda bread or crusty wholemeal/whole-wheat bread, lightly toasted (or a base of your choice – toasted English muffins also work well, see page 16)
2 ripe avocados, halved, pitted/stoned and peeled
black pepper, to season

serves 4

Poach the eggs to your liking following the instructions on page 10. Drain just before serving.

Meanwhile, put the chorizo slices into a dry frying pan/skillet and set over medium heat. Fry for a minute or so on either side to release the oil and to warm through. Remove the pan from the heat.

variation

Another option is to finely dice the chorizo, lightly fry it, mix it with the crushed avocados and season with pepper. It is a little like a meaty take on guacamole. Spread the mixture on the toasted bread and top with a poached or even fried egg.

For each open sandwich, drizzle a little olive oil on the toasted bread (or spread with butter, if you prefer). Crush half an avocado onto it using a fork, then layer two chorizo slices on top of the avocado. Place a poached egg on top, sprinkle some black pepper over and serve immediately.

Alternatively, serve the chorizo guacamole in a bowl with the poached egg on top and with toast soldiers on the side for dipping.

A hearty pork burger with all the traditional breakfast trimmings – for the days when cereal, or even a full English Breakfast, just won't cut it.

the big breakfast burger with Portobello mushroom & fried egg

2 tablespoons olive oil

5 mushrooms, finely chopped

200 g/7 oz. lean minced/ ground pork

2 teaspoons tomato ketchup, plus extra to serve

a pinch of mustard powder

3 tablespoons fresh breadcrumbs

a pinch each of sea salt and black pepper

2 eggs

2 Portobello mushrooms

2 English muffins (or Gluten-free English Muffins, see page 16)

serves 2

Heat 1 tablespoon of the oil in a frying pan/skillet set over medium heat. Add the chopped mushrooms and fry until soft and brown. Remove from the heat and set aside to cool.

Put the pork in a bowl with the tomato ketchup, mustard powder, breadcrumbs and salt and pepper. Work together with your hands until evenly mixed. Add the cooled mushrooms and mix again. Divide the mixture in half and shape into two burger patties. Press each burger down to make them nice and flat.

Heat the remaining oil in the same frying pan/skillet and fry the burgers over medium–high heat for 5 minutes on each side until cooked through. Keep warm.

Fry the eggs to your liking following the instructions on page 11 and grill/broil the Portobello mushrooms under medium heat.

Slice the English muffins in half and lightly toast them under a medium grill/broiler or in the toaster. Spread a spoonful of tomato ketchup on the base of each muffin and put the cooked burgers on top. Put a fried egg and a grilled/broiled Portobello mushroom on top of each burger and finish with the lids of the muffins.

Serve with extra tomato ketchup on the side.

These muffins encapsulate the main elements of a classic English fried breakfast, with bacon, tomatoes and a whole egg on top. They are best served straight from the oven while still warm. Use high-sided muffin cases, which can hold the egg, and don't overfill with the muffin mixture, otherwise your eggs will spill over.

breakfast muffins

30 g/1 oz. crispy cooked smoked bacon rashers/slices
60 g/4 tablespoons butter, softened
1 tablespoon caster/granulated sugar
1 large hen's egg, plus 6 small hen's (or quail) eggs
45 g/⅓ cup gluten-free self-raising/rising flour (or 40 g/⅓ cup gluten-free plain/all-purpose flour plus ½ teaspoon baking powder and ¼ teaspoon xanthan gum)
15 g/2 tablespoons ground almonds
15 g/2 tablespoons fine cornmeal
1 tablespoon crème fraîche (or sour cream)
6 cherry vine tomatoes, halved
sea salt and black pepper, to season

a 6-hole muffin pan lined with 6 high-sided muffin cases

makes 6

Preheat the oven to 180°C (350°F) Gas 4.

Reserve 6 small strips of bacon to decorate the muffins and blitz the remaining bacon to fine crumbs in a food processor.

In a large mixing bowl, whisk together the butter, sugar, large hen's egg and the bacon crumbs. Add the flour (plus baking powder and xanthan gum, if using), almonds, cornmeal and crème fraîche (or sour cream), then whisk well so that everything is incorporated. Season with salt and pepper and stir.

Place a large spoonful of the batter into each of the muffin cases and top with two cherry tomato halves. Cover the tomatoes with another spoonful of batter, then carefully crack one of the small hen's or quail eggs into a bowl. Pour it onto the top of one of the muffins, taking care that it doesn't spill over the edge of the case (hold back a little of the egg white if the case is close to overflowing). Repeat with the remaining eggs and muffins. Sprinkle a little black pepper over each egg and lay one of the reserved bacon strips on top of each muffin.

Bake the muffins in the preheated oven for 15–20 minutes and serve straight away.

One for the veggies. Mushrooms in cream is an irresistible combination. A few thickly sliced tomatoes, quickly seared in some butter and oil in a pan, make a nice accompaniment, as does a fried egg or two. Or go one step further and crack your egg into a giant Portobello mushroom – the perfect vessel for a morning egg.

mushrooms & egg on toast with fried tomatoes

1 tablespoon butter
2–3 tablespoons vegetable oil
500 g/1 lb. button mushrooms, quartered or sliced
3–4 medium tomatoes, thickly sliced
2 eggs
1 garlic clove, crushed (optional)
a handful of fresh flat-leaf parsley, chopped
150 ml/⅔ cup single/light cream
4 slices wholemeal/ whole-wheat toast
sea salt and black pepper, to season

Portobello egg cups
(optional)
4 Portobello mushrooms, stalks removed and chopped, cup left whole

serves 2

Heat the butter and oil together in a frying pan/skillet over low–medium heat. Add the mushrooms and cook for about 10 minutes, stirring occasionally, until tender and golden. Season with salt and pepper to taste.

Meanwhile, set a grill pan over medium heat, add a little vegetable oil and carefully place the sliced tomatoes in the pan, starting at the top and working around the outside of the pan in a clockwise direction to help you know which slice to turn over in order (so you don't have some burnt or underdone tomatoes). Turn the slices once and cook on the other side.

Fry the eggs to your liking following the instructions on page 11.

Returning to the mushrooms, stir in the garlic (if using) and chopped parsley and cook for about 1 minute, then add the cream and simmer gently for 2–3 minutes. Taste and adjust the seasoning if necessary.

Serve immediately on toast with the fried tomatoes and eggs.

Portobello egg cups

For a twist on sliced mushrooms on toast, you could super-size this dish by using Portobello mushrooms instead of button mushrooms.

Prepare the sauce for the mushrooms as above, replacing the sliced button mushrooms with the chopped Portobello stalks.

Preheat a grill/broiler to medium and lay the mushrooms stalk-side down on a grill pan. Grill/broil the mushrooms for 1 minute then turn over and spoon a little of the sauce into the well of each mushroom. Crack an egg directly on top and return to the grill/ broiler. Cook until the white of the egg is cooked through and the yolk is still slightly runny.

Serve with or without toast (soldiers work well here) with any remaining sauce drizzled over the top.

The batter for these classic American pancakes makes platefuls of light and fluffy pancakes from just one egg. Served with lashings of maple syrup and whipped maple butter, this is an indulgent yet cheap breakfast. Alternatively, serve these pancakes with crispy bacon in place of the maple butter – the sweet and salty combination is delicious.

pancake stack with whipped maple butter

160 g/1¼ cups self-raising/rising flour, sifted
1 teaspoon baking powder
1 egg, separated
1 teaspoon vanilla extract
60 g/scant ⅓ cup caster/granulated sugar
a pinch of salt
250 ml/1 cup whole milk
3 tablespoons melted butter, plus extra for frying

whipped maple butter
115 g/1 stick butter
60 ml/¼ cup maple syrup, plus extra to serve
60 g/½ cup icing/confectioners' sugar, sifted

mini choc-chip pancakes (optional)
100 g/⅔ cup chocolate chips
icing/confectioners' sugar, for dusting

serves 4

To make the pancake batter, put the flour, baking powder, egg yolk, vanilla extract, caster/granulated sugar, salt and milk in a large mixing bowl and whisk together. Add the melted butter and whisk again. The batter should have a smooth, dropping consistency.

In a separate bowl, whisk the egg white to stiff peaks. Gently fold the whisked egg white into the batter using a spatula. Cover and rest in the fridge for 30 minutes.

For the whipped maple butter, whisk together the butter, maple syrup and icing/confectioners' sugar using an electric handheld whisk until light and creamy. This is best made shortly before serving.

When you are ready to serve, remove the batter mixture from the fridge and stir once. Put a little butter in a large frying pan/skillet set over medium heat. Allow the butter to melt and coat the base of the pan, then ladle small amounts of the batter into the pan, leaving a little space between each pancake, or, if you want to make larger pancakes, you can fill the pan to make one at a time. Cook until the underside of each pancake is golden brown and a few bubbles start to appear on the top – this will take about 2–3 minutes. Flip the pancakes over using a spatula and cook on the other side until golden brown.

Cook the remaining batter in the same way in batches until it is all used up, adding a little butter to the pan each time, if required.

Serve the pancakes in a stack with a little maple butter and a drizzle of maple syrup on top.

mini choc-chip pancakes

Prepare the pancake batter as above and when you are ready to fry, ladle mini spoonfuls of batter into the pan and sprinkle with the chocolate chips. Carefully spoon over a little more batter to cover. Cook on both sides as above, then dust liberally with icing/confectioners' sugar to serve.

These breakfast quesadillas are a complete departure from traditional Mexican ingredients. If you want to make them more authentic, replace the baked beans with refried beans. If you crave a Mexican breakfast, however, the breakfast burrito with its fresh salsa and satisfying guacamole is a fantastic way to start the day.

ham & egg breakfast quesadilla

4 slices thick ham
8 large flour tortillas
200 g/2 cups grated
   Cheddar or Monterey
   Jack cheese
a 400-g/14-oz. can baked
   beans in tomato sauce
1 tablespoon vegetable oil
4 tablespoons butter
4 large eggs

serves 4–6

Preheat the oven to 120°C (250°F) Gas ½.

To assemble the quesadillas, put a slice of ham on half of the tortillas. Sprinkle each with a quarter of the cheese and spoon over a quarter of the beans. Top each with a plain tortilla.

Heat the oil in a non-stick frying pan/skillet set over medium heat. When hot, add a quesadilla, lower the heat and cook for 2–3 minutes until golden on one side and the cheese begins to melt. Carefully turn over and cook the other side for 2–3 minutes. Transfer to a heatproof plate and keep warm in the preheated oven while you cook the other quesadillas.

Melt 1 tablespoon of the butter in a small non-stick frying pan/skillet. Add an egg and fry until cooked through, turning once to cook both sides if desired. Repeat to cook the remaining eggs.

Cut each quesadilla into wedges and top with a fried egg. Serve immediately while still warm.

breakfast burrito (pictured, page 5)

5 large eggs
1 large potato, cooked
   and diced
1 fresh red or green chilli/
   chile, finely chopped
2–3 spring onions/
   scallions, finely chopped
a small bunch fresh
   coriander/cilantro,
   finely chopped
1 teaspoon fine sea salt
2 tablespoons butter
75 g/scant 1 cup grated
   Cheddar cheese
2 large flour tortillas
1 avocado, thinly sliced
tomato salsa, to serve

serves 2

Put the eggs in a large bowl and whisk well. Stir in the diced potato, chilli/chile, spring onions/scallions, coriander/cilantro and salt.

Melt the butter in a large frying pan/skillet. Add the egg mixture and cook, stirring often, until the eggs are just set. Stir in the cheese, cook for 1 minute then transfer to a warmed plate for a moment.

To serve, divide the egg mixture between warmed tortillas and top with avocado slices. Fold the bottom up over most of the filling, then fold over the sides, overlapping to enclose the filling but leaving the burrito open at one end.

Serve immediately with tomato salsa and any excess ingredients on the side.

French toast, or 'eggy bread', is a simple way to use eggs to create a luxurious breakfast. Cinnamon is a versatile spice – it goes well in coffees, crumbles, cakes and cookies – and is used in abundance in this recipe as the bread is sandwiched together with a sweet cinnamon butter and the egg batter contains ground cinnamon. This French toast can be served with fresh berries or stewed apple if you wish.

cinnamon French toast

8 slices white bread
4 eggs
60 ml/¼ cup whole milk
2 teaspoons ground cinnamon
1 tablespoon caster/granulated sugar
1–2 tablespoons butter, for frying
sugar nibs/pearl sugar (or caster/granulated sugar), for sprinkling
icing/confectioners' sugar, to dust

cinnamon butter
100 g/7 tablespoons butter, softened
1 teaspoon vanilla sugar (see Cook's Note)
50 g/¼ cup caster/granulated sugar
2 teaspoons ground cinnamon

serves 4

For the cinnamon butter, mix together the butter, vanilla sugar, caster/granulated sugar and cinnamon to a smooth paste using the back of a spoon or fork.

Spread a thick layer of cinnamon butter over half of the slices of bread and place a second slice of bread on top of each to sandwich the butter in the middle. Press the sandwiches down so that the filling will not leak.

Whisk together the eggs, milk, cinnamon and caster/granulated sugar in a mixing bowl, transfer to a shallow dish and set aside. Melt the butter in a large frying pan/skillet set over medium heat until the butter begins to foam. Soak each sandwich in the egg mixture on one side for a few seconds, then turn over and soak the other side. The bread should be fully coated in egg, but not too soggy – it is best to soak one sandwich at a time.

Add the melted butter to the frying pan/skillet and put each sandwich straight into the pan before soaking the next sandwich. Sprinkle the tops of the sandwiches with sugar nibs/pearl sugar and cook for 2–3 minutes. Once the sandwiches are golden brown underneath, turn over and cook for a few minutes longer. The pearl sugar will caramelize and create a crusty topping. Keep the cooked toast warm while you cook the remaining slices in the same way, adding a little butter to the pan each time, if required.

Serve immediately, sliced and dusted with icing/confectioners' sugar.

cook's note
To prepare vanilla pods/beans for use in cooking, simply cut in half and run the back of a knife along the pod/bean halves to remove the seeds. Once used, the pod/bean can be washed, dried and then stored in a sterilized jar filled with caster/granulated sugar to make vanilla sugar.

There is nothing more satisfying than cracking the top of a soft-boiled/cooked egg with the back of a spoon, lifting off the top and revealing an oozing yolk ready for dipping bread soldiers into. Nothing, that is, unless it's dipping these bread biscuits in instead. They should be as light as a feather and the trick is to handle the dough as little as possible. If you are a vegetarian, you can use vegetable shortening to make them, but lard makes the very best biscuits.

bread biscuits with soft-boiled/cooked eggs

250 g/2 cups plain/all-purpose flour
2½ teaspoons baking powder
2 g/½ teaspoon salt
80 g/5 tablespoons cold lard (or vegetable shortening), cubed, plus extra, melted, to glaze
185 ml/¾ cup buttermilk, (or sour milk, or 50% plain yogurt and 50% whole milk)
10 soft-boiled/cooked eggs (see page 10)

a fluted cookie cutter
a baking sheet lined with baking parchment

serves 10 and makes about 30

Preheat the oven to 230°C (450°F) Gas 8.

Sift together the flour, baking powder and salt in a bowl. Add the lard (or vegetable shortening) and gradually rub between fingertips to the consistency of fine breadcrumbs.

Add the buttermilk (or sour milk, or yogurt-milk) and mix quickly with a fork until the mixture is just blended.

Pull the dough out onto a floured surface and knead lightly just to incorporate all the ingredients.

Gently roll out to a thickness of 5 cm/2 inches. Stamp out rounds with the cookie cutter, dipping the cutter in flour between each cut and making sure not to twist the cutter when you push it in or pull it out. Re-roll the off-cuts of dough and stamp out more rounds.

Arrange the biscuits on the prepared baking sheet and glaze the tops with melted lard (or vegetable shortening) for an even more savoury flavour.

Bake in the preheated oven for 12–15 minutes until golden on the outside and fluffy and soft on the inside. Remove from the oven and transfer to a wire rack to cool.

Serve 2–3 biscuits with each soft-boiled/cooked egg.

cook's note

Biscuits are one of the staples of soul food. Plain, simple, hearty, tasty and definitely fattening when not eaten in moderation. Soul food includes fried chicken, country ham, collard greens, fried okra, grits, pork sliders, pulled pork, hushpuppies, black-eyed peas… the list is endless and it's fine if you are working in the fields all day but not so fine if you have a desk job. Proceed with caution or just throw caution to the wind and enjoy!

Goat's cheese has a surprising affinity with eggs and makes for a delightful breakfast or brunch dish when whipped up as an omelette. Alternatively, the combination of sharp, yet creamy, sheep's cheese (pecorino) and the fresh, almost musky flavour of artichoke hearts is sublime and transforms an omelette into something truly sumptuous.

goat's cheese omelette with wild garlic/ramps & chervil (pictured)

a small handful of fresh chervil (or parsley)

3 eggs

2 wild garlic/ramps leaves, finely shredded, or some snipped fresh chives

1 tablespoon butter

15 g/½ oz. goat's cheese, crumbled

sea salt and black pepper, to season

mixed salad leaves, to serve

serves 1

Pick the chervil, cutting away the tougher stems, and finely chopping the leaves. Beat the eggs in a bowl with a splash of water (about 1 tablespoon), add the chopped chervil and wild garlic/ramps leaves, and beat again. Season lightly with salt and pepper.

Heat a medium frying pan/skillet until hot, add the butter, swirl it round, and pour in the beaten eggs and herbs, swirling them around too. Lift the edge of the omelette as it begins to cook, letting the liquid egg run from the centre to the edge. Scatter over the goat's cheese and leave for a minute to allow the omelette to brown. Add more pepper if you like. Fold one side of the omelette over and tip it onto a plate. You could serve this with some lightly dressed mixed salad leaves.

artichoke & pecorino omelette

12 medium purply-green artichokes with stems, heads about 10 cm/ 4 inches long

3 large ripe lemons

4 tablespoons extra virgin olive oil

6 large eggs

4 tablespoons chopped fresh parsley

4 tablespoons grated pecorino

sea salt and black pepper, to season

serves 2–4

First prepare the artichokes. Fill a big bowl with water, halve the lemons and squeeze in the juice of 4 halves to acidulate it. Use the remaining lemon halves to rub the cut portions of each artichoke as you work. Trim the artichokes by snapping off the dark green and purple outer leaves, starting at the base, and leaving only the pale interior leaves. Trim the stalk down to about 5 cm/2 inches in length. Trim away the dark green outer layer at the base and peel the fibrous outside of the stalk. Cut about 1 cm/⅜ inch off the tip of each artichoke. Put each artichoke in the lemony water until needed to stop them discolouring.

Drain the artichokes, halve them and pat dry with paper towels. Heat the oil in a large frying pan/skillet and sauté the artichokes for 5–10 minutes until tender and golden.

Beat the eggs in a bowl, add the parsley and season with salt and pepper. Put the pan back on the heat and pour the eggs around the artichokes. Cook over low heat until almost set. Scatter the pecorino on top and finish off under the grill/broiler. Serve warm or at room temperature.

The British invented bubble and squeak as a clever way to use leftover boiled dinner (boiled beef brisket, potato and cabbage). Americans dropped the cabbage and renamed it corned beef hash – a savoury, hearty breakfast dish. This brunch skillet doesn't use leftovers, but if you have any leftover beef brisket, be sure to try the corned beef hash.

steak & egg brunch skillet

1½ onions, chopped
2 carrots, chopped
3 sticks/ribs celery, sliced
1 garlic clove, halved and
   2 cloves, crushed
3 tablespoons tomato
   purée/paste
250 ml/1 cup red wine
2 litres/1¾ quarts chicken
   stock
4 tablespoons brown sugar
80 ml/⅓ cup
   Worcestershire sauce
2 tablespoons soy sauce
a handful of fresh thyme,
   plus extra to serve
3 bay leaves
4–5 beef thin/short rib(s),
   boneless, uncooked
120 g/½ cup potatoes,
   diced
1 shallot, finely diced
4 eggs
olive oil and butter, for
   frying
sea salt and black pepper,
   to season
flat-leaf parsley, to serve
mayonnaise (see page
   124), to serve

corned beef hash (optional)
700 g/1½ lbs. potatoes,
   diced
1 onion, diced
1 garlic clove, crushed
300 g/10½ oz. cooked
   corned beef brisket, diced
½ teaspoon Tabasco sauce
4 eggs

serves †

Preheat the oven to 150°C (300°F) Gas 2.

Add a little olive oil to an ovenproof frying pan/skillet and set over medium heat. Caramelize two-thirds of the onion, the carrots, celery and halved garlic. Add the tomato purée/paste and cook for 1–2 minutes. Add the red wine and reduce the mixture by half. Add the stock, brown sugar, Worcestershire sauce, soy sauce, thyme and bay leaves. Season generously with salt and pepper and bring to the boil. Add the thin/short rib(s) and transfer the pan to the preheated oven for 2 hours or until the meat is tender.

Remove the pan from the oven, strain and reserve the liquid and discard the vegetables and herbs. Over medium heat, boil the reserved liquid, skim off the fat and reduce until it coats the back of a spoon. Set this braising liquid aside.

corned beef hash

Boil and fry the potatoes as above. Add the onion, garlic and corned beef. Season and sauté for 5 minutes. Pour the mixture into the bowl with the potatoes. Add the Tabasco and mix well.

Add a little more butter to the frying pan/skillet. Pour the potato mixture into it and press everything down firmly. Cover with a heavy lid or

For the hash, bring a pan of water to a boil. Blanch the potatoes until tender. Drain and run them under cold water to stop from cooking. Heat a knob/pat of butter in a frying pan/skillet over medium heat, add the potatoes and fry until lightly brown. Set aside. Add a little olive oil to the pan and return to medium heat. Caramelize the remaining onion, add the shallot and crushed garlic, and continue cooking until the mixture is golden.

Dice the thin/short rib(s), and add the potatoes, onion, shallot and garlic. Add the reserved braising liquid to moisten and mix in the thyme, parsley and potatoes. Season to taste, return to the pan and keep warm.

Fry the eggs following the instructions on page 11. Serve with a fried egg on top and mayonnaise on the side.

plate that will fit just inside the pan to weigh the mixture down. Cook over medium heat for 10 minutes. Turn the mixture over and cook for 10 minutes on the other side. The meat should be brown and crisp. Make indentations in the potatoes and crack an egg into each one. Place a fitted lid over the pan and cook until the eggs are done.

This timeless recipe features simple ingredients, carefully cooked, with a little spicy twist. It really is hard to go wrong with a tortilla or 'Spanish omelette'. Eaten hot or cold, it is welcome at any time of day. It is worth remembering that this is not anything like a French omelette; it requires comparatively long and gentle cooking. Like the Italian frittata (see page 99) it is, however, always worth the wait.

Spanish omelette

50 ml/3 tablespoons olive
  oil
2 large white onions,
  thinly sliced
2 large potatoes, peeled
  and thinly sliced
4 roasted Piquillo peppers
  (see Cook's Note),
  roughly chopped
6 eggs
sea salt and black pepper,
  to season
green salad, to serve

serves †

Heat half the oil in a large, heavy-based frying pan/skillet, add the onions and potatoes and toss to coat. Season well and add the Piquillo peppers. Turn down the heat and cover with a lid. Cook until the potatoes and onions are soft and translucent, about 20 minutes. Turn regularly to prevent too much browning. Once they are softened, remove them from the oil with a slotted spoon and set aside.

Lightly whisk the eggs in a large mixing bowl and add the onions and potatoes (they should still be hot so that the cooking process of the eggs begins as soon as they are mixed together). Season with salt and pepper. Add the rest of the oil to the pan and return to medium heat. Pour the egg mixture into the hot pan – it should fill it by about two-thirds. Turn the heat down to its lowest setting and cook for 20–25 minutes until there is very little liquid on the surface.

Take a plate that is slightly larger than the frying pan/skillet and place it upside down over the pan. Invert the

plate and pan, tipping the tortilla out onto the plate. Put the pan back on the heat and gently slide the tortilla back into it. The cooked side is now facing upward and the uncooked side will now be on the heat. Cook for a further 2–3 minutes.

Turn off the heat and let settle. (If you don't feel up to flipping the tortilla over, you can grill/broil the top for 2–3 minutes under medium heat to finish off.)

Turn the tortilla out onto a clean plate and slice to serve. This is great with a green salad and a glass of good Spanish Rioja.

cook's note

Fresh Piquillo peppers come from northern Spain and are harvested in September and December. You can roast them (preferably over an open fire or barbecue) and peel the skin off for this recipe. Ready-roasted peppers are available from good Spanish importers, peeled and packed into delicious Spanish olive oil.

The simple omelette is one of the best ways to use up leftover cold roast ham. Even the shredded bits left on the board are perfect for the omelette mixture – just throw everything in!

roast ham omelette

6 eggs
25 ml/1½ tablespoons
   whole milk
1 tablespoon freshly
   chopped parsley
a small pinch of mustard
   powder
a handful of cooked ham,
   chopped or shredded
a handful of mature
   Cheddar cheese, cubed
   (optional)
20 g/generous 1
   tablespoon butter
sea salt and black pepper,
   to season

serves 2

Crack the eggs into a bowl and beat them really well, then add the milk, parsley and mustard powder, season with salt and pepper, and mix again. Throw in the ham and cubes of Cheddar cheese, if using.

Heat the butter in a frying pan/skillet over fairly high heat until it is fully melted and the pan is very hot. Pour in the egg mixture, pushing any away from the sides of the pan. Turn the heat right down and let the omelette cook slowly.

Once the bottom half of the omelette is solid, use a heatproof spatula to flip one side over. Cook until the eggs are set. Alternatively, leave the omelette flat and finish it under a hot grill/broiler.

Serve immediately.

cook's notes

• Make an omelette light and fluffy by separating the eggs and folding whisked egg whites into lightly beaten egg yolks before cooking.
• If you over-cook an omelette, let it cool then chop it up. Combine with mayonnaise and fresh chives, if desired, and use as a sandwich filling.

There are many versions of this Middle Eastern dish on breakfast menus in cafés around the world. Ensuring there is plenty of sauce helps to cook the eggs and provides lots of juice to mop up with bread.

baked eggs with chorizo, mushrooms & lemon crème fraîche

4 eggs
sea salt and black pepper, to season
Turkish bread, to serve

chorizo sauce
1 tablespoon olive oil
1 small red onion, finely chopped
2 garlic cloves, thinly sliced
120 g/4 oz. chorizo, cut into ½-cm/¼-inch slices
400 g/2 cups canned plum tomatoes
1 tablespoon balsamic vinegar
1½ teaspoons soft brown sugar
¼ teaspoon dried chilli/ hot red pepper flakes
½ star anise
1 strip orange peel, pith removed
12 basil leaves, roughly torn

baked mushrooms
15 g/1 tablespoon butter, plus extra for greasing
1 tablespoon olive oil
1 garlic clove, thinly sliced
4 Portobello mushrooms, sliced

lemon crème fraîche
150 g/½ cup crème fraîche (or sour cream)
¼ teaspoon grated lemon zest
½ teaspoon freshly squeezed lemon juice

a baking sheet, greased

serves 4

Begin by preparing the chorizo sauce. Put the oil in a large heavy-bottomed frying pan/skillet set over low–medium heat and gently sauté the chopped onion for 7–10 minutes until soft and translucent, but not coloured. Add the sliced garlic and chorizo, and cook until the chorizo starts to brown and release its oils. Add 60 ml/¼ cup of water and all the remaining ingredients except the basil. Season with salt and pepper, turn up the heat and bring the mixture to a boil. Immediately reduce the heat and simmer for 20–30 minutes, until the sauce is thick and glossy. Remove from the heat, discard the star anise and orange rind, stir in the basil and set aside.

Preheat the oven to 180°C (350°F) Gas 4.

To prepare the mushrooms, melt the butter and olive oil in a frying pan/skillet set over medium heat. Add the sliced garlic and allow it to cook gently for 2–3 minutes, then remove the pan from the heat. Arrange the mushrooms on the prepared baking sheet and spoon over the garlic-infused butter. Cover with foil and bake in the preheated oven for 15–20 minutes until tender.

To make the lemon crème fraîche, combine all of the ingredients in a bowl, cover and set aside.

Return the chorizo sauce to low heat and gently reheat. Add the baked mushrooms to the pan, making sure they are evenly distributed and half-submerged in the sauce. Make four holes in the sauce with a wooden spoon and crack in the eggs. Cover and cook very gently for 15–20 minutes until the whites are set and the yolks still a little runny. Sprinkle with black pepper and serve with Turkish bread and the lemon crème fraîche.

Fishcakes are a complete meal – fish and herby potatoes in one convenient parcel. They need only a simple salad on the side for the perfect brunch. The creamy yolk of the poached egg mixed with potato is pretty special and there's added eggy goodness in the dill mayo.

smoked haddock fishcakes with poached eggs & dill mayo

4 large Maris Piper, King Edward or other floury potatoes
300 ml/1¼ cups whole milk
1 bay leaf
400 g/14 oz. undyed smoked haddock
25 g/½ cup finely chopped fresh chives
20 g/scant ½ cup finely chopped fresh dill
25 g/2 tablespoons melted butter
1 egg, lightly beaten, plus 6 for poaching
vegetable oil, for frying
sea salt and black pepper, to season

dill mayo
200 ml/¾ cup mayonnaise
1 tablespoon chopped dill
½ teaspoon grated lemon zest
1 tablespoon lemon juice

to serve
a bunch of fresh watercress
2 tablespoons olive oil
freshly squeezed juice of 1 lemon

a baking sheet lined with clingfilm/plastic wrap

serves 6

Put the whole potatoes (with the skin on) in a large pot filled with water set over medium–high heat. Boil for 20–25 minutes, or until cooked through. Drain and transfer to a plate to cool. Cover and chill in the fridge for at least 2 hours, or preferably overnight. This process of boiling the potatoes whole and refrigerating them removes a lot of their moisture, which prevents the fishcakes from falling apart.

To prepare the haddock, put the milk and bay leaf in a large frying pan/skillet set over medium heat and bring to a boil. Add the haddock, skin-side down. Reduce the heat and simmer for 3 minutes. Flip the fillets over, turn off the heat and allow the haddock to continue to cook in the residual heat.

Grate the chilled potatoes into a large mixing bowl – the skin should come away from the potato as you grate. Discard the skin and add the chopped herbs, melted butter, salt, pepper and beaten egg. Mix well.

Lift the haddock out of the milk, remove the skin and discard along with the milk. Flake the fish into chunks and add to the potato mixture. Stir gently to combine, taking care not to break up the fish pieces too much.

Form 12 round patties with your hands and place the fishcakes on the prepared baking sheet, cover with clingfilm/plastic wrap and set in the fridge for at least 1 hour to firm up.

When ready to serve, preheat the oven to 160°C (325°F) Gas 3 and put a large saucepan or pot of water with a pinch of salt over medium heat for poaching the eggs.

Heat 2 tablespoons of oil in a non-stick frying pan/skillet. Fry the fishcakes in batches for 3–4 minutes each side until lightly golden. Transfer to a clean baking sheet and keep warm in the oven while you cook the remaining fishcakes in the same way, adding more oil to the pan each time.

To poach the eggs, maintain the water at a gentle simmer. Crack an egg into a cup or ramekin and gently tip it into the pot. Repeat with the other eggs and cook in batches for 4 minutes. Drain on paper towels.

To make the dill mayo, mix all of the ingredients together and season to taste with salt and pepper.

Serve the fishcakes with a poached egg on top, the dill mayo and some fresh watercress dressed with a little olive oil and lemon juice.

When you take some of the components of a traditional 'English Breakfast' and prepare it like this, you can eat it for any meal in the day.

scrambled egg, roast tomatoes & prosciutto with mushroom purée

15 g/½ oz. dried porcini mushrooms (or 25 g/ 1 oz. fresh porcini mushrooms, finely chopped)
8 medium vine tomatoes
2 tablespoons olive oil
45 g/3 tablespoons butter
1 garlic clove, crushed
1 tablespoon crème fraîche (or sour cream)
a big pinch of freshly snipped chives
4 eggs
50 ml/scant ¼ cup whole milk
6 slices prosciutto
sea salt and black pepper, to season

serves 2

Preheat the oven to 190°C (375°F) Gas 5.

First, prepare the mushroom purée. If you're using dried porcini mushrooms, soak them in boiling water for about 20 minutes, then drain and finely chop.

While the mushrooms are soaking, prepare the roast tomatoes. Keep the tomatoes on the vine and put them in an ovenproof dish, then drizzle over the olive oil. Season with salt and pepper. Roast in the preheated oven for 20–25 minutes, until they are soft and start to brown.

Meanwhile, melt 15 g/1 tablespoon of the butter in a frying pan/skillet, then add the garlic and soaked or fresh porcini mushrooms. Mix in the crème fraîche (or sour cream) and stir well. Remove from the heat and keep hot. Sprinkle snipped chives on the top.

A few minutes before you are ready to serve, make the scrambled eggs. In a bowl, beat the eggs, milk and a bit of pepper together really well.

Melt the remaining 30 g/ 2 tablespoons butter in a separate frying pan/skillet and pour in the egg mixture, stirring constantly to keep it from setting or sticking. Continue cooking and stirring, until the eggs are scrambled to your liking.

You can serve the prosciutto slices as they are, or, lay the slices in the pan that you used for the mushroom purée and cook for just a couple of minutes on each side, turning once, so that they start to crisp and soak up some of the flavour of the mushrooms.

Serve the scrambled eggs immediately with the mushroom purée, roast tomatoes and prosciutto.

A classic Huevos Rancheros, made up of eggs, spices, tomatoes and salsa, wrapped up in flour tortillas, is given a gentle twist with Huevos con Chorizo. Mexican chorizo usually comes as ground meat but this recipe uses the Spanish sausage found in most supermarkets. Its deep reddish colour seeps out into the eggs to give them a lovely orange tint.

huevos con chorizo (pictured)

4 eggs
1 teaspoon olive oil
100 g/3½ oz. chorizo, thinly sliced
¼ onion, finely chopped
50 g/½ cup grated Monterey Jack or Cheddar cheese

to serve
flour tortillas
refried black or pinto beans
tomato salsa or hot sauce

serves 2

Break the eggs into a bowl and beat well with a fork.

Put the oil in a non-stick frying pan/skillet over medium heat – you only need a very small amount because the chorizo will release some of its own oil upon cooking.

Add the chorizo and fry for about 20 seconds, then add the onion and fry for another 20 seconds, stirring continuously.

Add the eggs and scramble, stirring to break up the eggs, for 1–2 minutes.

Remove from the heat and sprinkle the cheese over the top.

Serve with warm tortillas, refried beans and your favourite salsa or hot sauce if you dare.

huevos rancheros

½ tablespoon olive oil
8 slices of back or streaky bacon, finely chopped
1 large onion, finely chopped
1 garlic clove, crushed
4 hot green chillies/chiles, finely chopped
1 mild red chilli/chile, deseeded and finely chopped
4 tomatoes, skinned and roughly chopped
½ teaspoon sea salt
¼ teaspoon black pepper
8 eggs
4 flour tortillas
tomato salsa, to serve

serves 1

Heat the oil in a frying pan/skillet over medium heat and gently fry the bacon until almost cooked. Drain off all but 1 teaspoon of the fat.

Add the onion and garlic to the pan and cook, allowing it to lightly brown. Add the chillies/chiles, tomatoes, salt and pepper, stir well and cover. Bring to the boil, reduce the heat and simmer for about 20 minutes, stirring frequently.

Meanwhile, fry or poach the eggs to your taste following the instructions on pages 10–11 and gently warm the tortillas in a frying pan/skillet or warm oven, or under the grill/broiler.

To serve, place two eggs per person on a warmed tortilla and liberally spoon the salsa over the eggs.

The best thing is that these eggs don't require your full attention. Make the spiced ratatouille base and crack the eggs on top. Give the yolks a bonnet of yogurt and garlic, then bake. The cumin in this dish brings some dark murkiness to the table and the chilli/chile sings of warmth.

Moroccan baked eggs (pictured)

1½ teaspoons ground cumin
1 tablespoon olive oil
1 onion, thinly sliced
1 carrot, grated
1 teaspoon chopped red chilli/chile
1 red and 1 yellow (bell) pepper, cut into 1-cm/½-inch strips
2 teaspoons salt
2 eggs
2 tablespoons natural yogurt
1 garlic clove, grated
toasted pita bread, to serve

2 ramekins

serves 2

Preheat the oven to 180°C (350°F) Gas 4.

Toast the cumin in a dry frying pan/skillet over medium heat for 30 seconds until it smells nutty. Add the olive oil and onion, and fry until the onion is translucent.

Add the carrot, chilli/chile and (bell) pepper. Sauté for 5 minutes until the peppers have softened. Add 120 ml/½ cup water and turn the heat down to medium. Cook for about 15 minutes until the peppers and onions have relaxed into a gentle compote. You should end up with 250–350 ml/1–1½ cups compote. Season with salt.

Divide the mixture between the ramekins, making sure there is at least 2 cm/¾ inch clear at the top of each ramekin. Create a well in the centre of the compote with the back of a spoon. Crack an egg into the well, but be careful that the yolk doesn't break. Repeat for the other ramekins.

Float a tablespoon of yogurt over each egg yolk. Sprinkle half a teaspoon of grated garlic over the top and bake for about 15 minutes, until the whites are set, but the yolk is still runny.

Serve with toasted pita bread and fresh mint tea.

baked eggs with smoked mackerel

butter, for greasing
1 smoked mackerel fillet
2 tablespoons double/heavy cream
½ teaspoon Dijon mustard
2 eggs
freshly chopped flat-leaf parsley, chives or dill (optional)
black pepper, to season

2 ramekins, greased

serves 2

Preheat the oven to 180°C (350°F) Gas 4.

Put a baking sheet in the oven, ensuring there is enough room between the oven shelves for the baking sheet which will soon contain the ramekins.

Flake the mackerel into a bowl with the cream and mustard. Season with pepper and stir.

Put the mackerel mixture into the bottom of each greased ramekin. Crack the eggs, carefully depositing each egg into each ramekin on top of the mackerel. Open the oven, place the ramekins on the baking sheet, and pour boiling water around the ramekins so that it comes halfway up.

Check after 10 minutes. The egg white should be set, but the yolk still runny. If you'd rather have your egg more cooked, put it back in the oven for a few more minutes. Once ready, scatter with chopped herbs and serve.

cook's note

Smoked mackerel is delicious, distinctive and cheap. It keeps for ages in the fridge and is packed with Omega-3s, so there's really no eggs-cuse not to try these baked eggs.

Here are all the flavours of a traditional full farmhouse English fry-up in a quiche. Bake it the day before a long, early-morning journey when you need a quick on-the-go breakfast.

English breakfast quiche

225 g/1¾ cups plain/all-purpose flour
1 teaspoon English mustard powder
150 g/1 stick plus 3 tablespoons butter, chilled and cubed
1 egg, beaten

filling
4 pork sausages
200 g/7 oz. cherry tomatoes, halved
200 g/7 oz. bacon lardons
200 g/7 oz. button mushrooms, halved
1 tablespoon olive oil
300 ml/1½ cups crème fraîche (or sour cream)
3 large eggs, beaten
1 teaspoon English mustard powder

a 25-cm/10-inch fluted, loose-bottomed tart pan
baking beans

serves 6

Preheat the oven to 200°C (400°F) Gas 6.

To make the pastry, put the flour, mustard powder and butter in a food processor and pulse until they are just combined. Add the egg and run the motor until the mixture just comes into a ball. Turn out, wrap with clingfilm/plastic wrap and chill in the fridge for 30 minutes.

To make the filling, put the sausages in a roasting dish and roast in the preheated oven for 10 minutes. Take the dish out of the oven, throw in the tomatoes, bacon and mushrooms, drizzle over the oil and return to the oven to roast for 15–20 minutes, until everything is tender and cooked through. Remove the dish but leave the oven on.

Roll out the pastry on a lightly floured surface until it is about 3-mm/⅛-inch thick and use to line the tart pan. Press the pastry into the corners and leave the overhang. Prick the base all over with a fork, line with baking parchment and fill with baking beans. Bake in the oven for 8 minutes, then remove the beans and baking parchment. Trim off the overhang and reduce the heat to 150°C (300°F) Gas 2. Return the pastry case to the oven for 2–3 minutes to dry out while you finish the filling.

Slice the sausages and scatter them with the rest of the roasted ingredients into the pastry case. Mix the crème fraîche, eggs and mustard powder and pour over everything in the pastry case.

Bake for 30–35 minutes, until set around the edges. Turn off the oven and leave the tart to cool in the oven, with the door open for at least 15 minutes. Cut into slices and serve warm or cold.

Bubble and squeak is a classic breakfast invention that transforms leftover roast vegetables with an added fried egg for the ultimate fry up.

bubble & squeak with pear & apple chutney

30 g/2 tablespoons butter

1 onion, sliced

1 garlic clove, finely chopped

¼ white cabbage, shredded

400 g/2 cups mashed potato

500 g/2½ cups roast vegetables (squash, carrot and parsnip)

15 g/¼ cup freshly chopped flat-leaf parsley

black pudding, thickly sliced and grilled

4 fried eggs (see page 11)

Pear & Apple Chutney (or store-bought chutney)

sea salt and black pepper, to season

serves 4

pear & apple chutney
(optional)

100 ml/⅓ cup vegetable oil

2 small red onions, finely diced

7 apples, finely diced

7 pears, finely diced

250 g/1¼ cups soft brown sugar

250 g/1¼ cups dark brown sugar

200 ml/¾ cup red wine vinegar

10 g/2 tablespoons ground ginger

5 g/1 tablespoon ground coriander

5 g/1 tablespoon ground allspice

sterilized glass jars with airtight lids

makes 1.5 litres/quarts

Melt the butter in a non-stick frying pan/skillet set over low–medium heat. Add the onion and garlic and cook for about 10 minutes, until soft and caramelized. Add the shredded cabbage and sweat down for 2–3 minutes. Add the mashed potato, other roast vegetables, parsley, salt and pepper, and mix well. Cook for a further 15–20 minutes, turning the vegetables from time to time and using a spatula to flatten the vegetables onto the base of the pan so that they catch and get a crispy bottom.

Serve with a fried egg, thick slices of grilled black pudding and some chutney.

pear & apple chutney

Heat the oil in a heavy-bottomed saucepan or pot set over low heat. Sauté the onions, apples and pears until the onions are translucent. Add the remaining ingredients and simmer gently until the fruit is soft and the liquid has evaporated.

While still warm, spoon the chutney into sterilized, glass jars and, if not using straight away, seal and store. Carefully tap them on the counter to get rid of any air pockets, wipe clean and tightly screw on the lids. Turn the jars upside down and leave until completely cold. Store unopened for up to 6 months or in the fridge once opened for up to 2 months.

For a real taste of Madrid, this recipe takes the formula of pairing tomato bread with jamón and gilds it further, with fried eggs and some sneaky fries. For the ultimate indulgence, wrap one of the potato chips in ham and puncture the egg yolk with it. Then use the tomato bread to mop up the excess. If bliss has a taste, this could be it.

fried egg, tomato bread, jamón & fries

300 g/10 oz. floury
   potatoes
250 ml/1 cup sunflower
   (or canola) oil, for frying
2 tomatoes
2 garlic cloves
2 tablespoons olive oil,
   plus extra for frying
2 eggs
4 slices sourdough bread,
   toasted
2 pinches of sea salt
100 g/3½ oz. jamón
   Ibérico

serves 2

Trim the potatoes into squarish shapes (don't bother to peel them). Cut into fries 1-cm/¾-inch thick and dry well on paper towels.

Heat the sunflower oil in a deep pan or deep-fat fryer to 140°C (275°F). Make sure the oil is at least 3 cm/1¼ inches deep. Cook the fries for 4 minutes, scoop out and drain on paper towels.

While the fries are cooking, make the tomato bread. Grate the tomatoes using a sharp grater into a bowl. Some of the skin won't go through, but that's okay – you want a mushy pulp. Grate in 1 garlic clove. Whisk in the olive oil and season with a good pinch of salt.

Dry the fries well on paper towels, turn up the heat to 180°C (350°F)

and fry for another 3–4 minutes until golden and crisp. Remove and dry on paper towels and season well with another good pinch of salt.

Fry the eggs in a little olive oil until the whites are cooked and the yolks are still runny (see page 11).

Cut the remaining garlic clove in half and rub the cut side over the sourdough toast while it is still hot. Top with the tomato mush.

Serve the fries, fried eggs and tomato bread with the jamón. The tomato bread is also spectacular as a snack or starter/appetizer with a platter of cured meats.

A well-cooked steak with a rosy interior and charred exterior truly is a wonderful thing. Adorn it with a butter spiked with the piquant flavour of mustard and tarragon. When the steak is ready, it is clamped in a soft white bap slathered in this delicious butter, which will melt with the steak's residual heat. Along with a fried egg cooked so it is only just runny inside, this is one sandwich that you need to eat quickly before the egg and butter have time to trickle down your chin.

steak & fried egg baps with mustard butter

100 g/7 tablespoons butter, softened
2 teaspoons wholegrain mustard
½ teaspoon English mustard powder
1 tablespoon chopped fresh tarragon leaves
1 teaspoon Gentleman's relish or anchovy paste (optional)
2 white baps, halved horizontally
2 x 250-g/9-oz. rib-eye (or sirloin) steaks, roughly 1.5-cm/½-inch thick
3 tablespoons olive oil
2 large eggs
sea salt and black pepper, to season

serves 2

Put the butter in a mixing bowl and beat it with a spoon until squished against the sides of the bowl. Spoon in the wholegrain mustard, mustard powder, tarragon and relish, if using. Season to taste, taking care not to over-season as the relish will already be salty. Beat everything together and use to butter the insides of the baps.

Preheat a grill pan over high heat until very hot. Brush the steaks with 1 tablespoon of the oil and season well with salt and pepper. Using tongs, lay the steaks on the pan and press down. Leave them to cook for 2–4 minutes on each side. Press the centre of the steak to determine how well cooked it is. A light yield means it is medium, while anything soft is still rare. Transfer the steaks to a board and cut off any large pieces of fat. Leave to rest for 2–3 minutes while you cook the eggs.

Add the remaining oil to a frying pan/skillet and heat over high heat. Crack in the eggs and turn the heat to low. Cook for 2 minutes, then flip over for 30 seconds to cook the other side but leave the yolk with a bit of ooze. Place a fried egg in each bap and finish off with a steak.

This classic North African dish makes an excellent brunch to share. Serve it with homemade sun-dried tomato and rosemary cornbread or a fresh crusty baguette for mopping up the spiced tomato sauce.

Tunisian baked eggs in tomato sauce

450 g/1 lb. ripe tomatoes
1 tablespoon olive oil
1 onion, chopped
1 red (bell) pepper,
  chopped into strips
1 garlic clove, chopped
1 teaspoon ground cumin
½ teaspoon harissa
1 teaspoon brown sugar
4 eggs
sea salt and black pepper,
  to season
chopped fresh coriander/
  cilantro, to garnish

serves 4

Roughly chop the tomatoes, reserving the juices.

Heat the olive oil in a large, heavy-bottomed frying pan/skillet set over medium heat. Add the onion, (bell) pepper and garlic and fry, stirring often, for 5 minutes, until softened.

Mix together the cumin with 1 tablespoon of water in a small bowl to form a paste. Add the harissa and cumin paste to the pan and fry, stirring, for a minute. Add the tomatoes and

brown sugar, season with salt and pepper, and mix well. Bring to a boil, reduce the heat, cover and simmer for 5 minutes.

Uncover and simmer for a further 10 minutes, stirring now and then, to reduce and thicken the mixture.

Break the eggs, spaced well apart, into the tomato mixture. Cover and cook over low heat for 10 minutes until the eggs are set. Sprinkle with coriander/cilantro and serve at once.

sun-dried tomato & rosemary cornbread

130 g/1 cup plain/all-
  purpose flour
130 g/1 cup fine cornmeal
2 tablespoons white sugar
2 teaspoons baking
  powder
½ teaspoon salt
200 ml/¾ cup whole milk
2 eggs
50 g/3 tablespoons butter,
  melted
6 sun-dried tomatoes in
  oil, chopped into pieces
1 teaspoon finely
  chopped fresh rosemary

a 20-cm/8-in. square baking
pan, greased and foil-lined

makes 1 loaf

Preheat the oven to 200°C (400°F) Gas 6.

Mix the flour, cornmeal, sugar, baking powder and salt together in a large mixing bowl.

In a separate bowl, whisk together the milk and eggs, and stir in the melted butter.

Pour the milk and egg mixture into the flour mixture and add in the sun-dried tomatoes and rosemary. Quickly fold together, taking care not to over-mix.

Transfer the mixture to the prepared baking pan and bake in the preheated oven for 30 minutes, until risen and golden-brown.

Serve at once, warm from the oven.

This classic Anglo-Indian breakfast dish is great whatever time of day you choose to make it. The combination of flaked fish, hard-boiled/cooked eggs and spiced rice is both filling and full of flavour. Add as much or as little fresh chilli/chile as you dare.

kedgeree

450 g/1 lb. undyed
    smoked haddock fillets
2 bay leaves
120 g/¾ cup basmati rice
3 tablespoons olive oil
5 spring onions/scallions,
    finely chopped
1–2 garlic cloves, finely
    chopped
1–1½ tablespoons curry
    powder
freshly squeezed juice of
    1 lemon
2 hard-boiled/cooked
    eggs (see page 10)
2 tablespoons chopped
    fresh coriander/cilantro
black pepper, to season
lemon wedges, to serve
    (optional)

serves 4

Put the smoked haddock, bay leaves and 100 ml/⅓ cup of water in a frying pan/skillet and bring to a boil. Cover, reduce the heat and simmer for 5 minutes. Remove the pan from the heat, drain and, when cool enough to handle, remove the skin from the fish and flake the flesh with a fork. Set aside.

Meanwhile, bring a large saucepan of water to a boil. Add the rice and return to the boil. Stir, then reduce the heat and simmer for 10 minutes, until the rice is cooked but still has a slight bite to it. Drain and reserve.

Heat a large, non-stick frying pan/skillet. Add the oil, spring onions/scallions and garlic and fry gently until softened and slightly coloured, about 6 minutes. Add the curry powder and cook for 2 minutes. Add the lemon juice, reserved haddock and rice. Cut one egg into wedges and reserve. Chop the other one into small pieces and add to the pan. Sprinkle with the coriander/cilantro and season to taste with pepper. Continue to heat, stirring gently, until piping hot.

Transfer the kedgeree to a warm serving dish. Top with the reserved egg and lemon wedges (if using) and serve immediately.

variation

Use 400 g/14 oz. fresh salmon fillets instead of the haddock and cook as above. Alternatively, add 75 g/3 oz. smoked salmon, cut into thin strips, at the same time as the chopped egg.

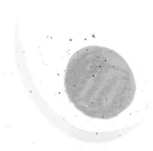

A classic Turkish dish, this colourful version of scrambled eggs is great for a flavourful breakfast or brunch. Serve menemen with rustic bread, a crisp baguette or toast.

menemen

200 g/7 oz. ripe tomatoes
6 eggs
½ teaspoon Turkish pepper flakes, such as Aleppo pepper
1 teaspoon fresh thyme leaves
7 g/½ tablespoon butter
1 tablespoon olive oil
2 spring onions/scallions, chopped
½ green (bell) pepper, chopped
2 teaspoons tomato purée/paste
2 tablespoons chopped fresh flat-leaf parsley
sea salt and black pepper, to season

serves 1

Begin by scalding the tomatoes. Pour boiling water over the ripe tomatoes in a heatproof bowl. Set aside for 1 minute, then drain and carefully peel off the skin using a sharp knife. Roughly chop, reserving any juices, and set aside.

Beat the eggs in a large mixing bowl and season with the Turkish pepper flakes, thyme, salt and pepper.

Heat the butter and oil in a large, heavy-bottomed frying pan/skillet set over low heat. Add the spring onions/scallions and (bell) pepper and fry gently, stirring, for 2 minutes. Add the chopped tomatoes and cook, stirring often, for 8–10 minutes, until the tomatoes have softened and form a thick paste. Add the tomato purée/paste, mixing in well.

Pour in the beaten, seasoned eggs and gently stir. Cook, stirring gently now and then, until the eggs are to your taste.

Garnish with fresh parsley and serve at once.

If you are having friends over for Sunday brunch, these glorious hash browns should be served with a Bloody Mary. The kimchi takes a week to ferment at home or can be store-bought. Topped with gooey poached eggs and sprinkled with aromatic herbs, Sunday couldn't be better.

spicy kimchi hash browns with poached eggs

1 large Russet potato, grated with skin on
2 garlic cloves, crushed
160 g/2 cups Spicy Kimchi (see below)
3 tablespoons olive oil, plus extra to serve
4 eggs
1 tablespoon vinegar
a bunch of fresh Thai basil
a small bunch of fresh flat-leaf parsley, torn
sea salt and black pepper, to season
hot sauce, to serve

spicy kimchi

1 small Napa cabbage and 1 small Savoy cabbage, halved and cored
150 g/¾ cup sea salt
3 carrots, grated
4 spring onions/scallions, thinly sliced
a 5-cm/2-inch piece of ginger, peeled and grated
4 radishes, grated
2 Persian cucumbers, grated
120 ml/½ cup rice wine vinegar
2 tablespoons fish sauce
2 tablespoons sambal oelek chile paste

serves 1

Put the grated potato, garlic and kimchi in a large bowl and mix together. Season with salt and pepper.

Heat a large cast-iron frying pan/skillet over medium–high heat and add the olive oil. When the oil starts to sizzle, add the potato-kimchi mix and brown for 2 minutes. Reduce the heat and continue to cook, stirring occasionally, for another 6–8 minutes. You want the hash browns to be crispy and browned.

Crack the eggs into separate small bowls. Fill a medium frying pan/skillet three-quarters of the way up with water. Add a tablespoon of vinegar and place over medium heat until bubbles start to form in the bottom. Carefully pour the eggs one at a time into the water, making sure they are spaced apart. Cook for 4 minutes, then remove with a slotted spoon, gently shaking off any excess water.

Divide the hash browns between plates or serving skillets and top each with an egg. Scatter with torn Thai basil and parsley, drizzle with a little olive oil and finish with a sprinkle of salt and pepper. Serve with hot sauce.

spicy kimchi

Slice the cabbages into 2.5-cm/1-inch strips and put in a large ceramic bowl. Dissolve the salt in 1.4 litres/quarts water and pour over the cabbage. Cover with clingfilm/plastic wrap and let stand at room temperature for 8–24 hours.

Drain the cabbage and place back in the bowl with the carrots, spring onions/scallions, ginger, radishes, and cucumbers. Add the vinegar, fish sauce, sambal oelek chile paste, and 120 ml/½ cup water, and mix. Spoon the cabbage mixture into sterilized glass jars and pour over any remaining juice. Screw the lids on tightly and let the jars sit at room temperature for 24 hours. Refrigerate for at least 5 days before serving. It will keep in the fridge for up to 6 weeks.

In French cooking, dishes served on a bed of spinach are called 'a la florentine', and so it is that these baked eggs, spiked with nutmeg and layered with spinach, are too.

florentine baked eggs (pictured)

225 g/3½ cups young-leaf
  spinach, rinsed
4 very fresh eggs
4 dessertspoons virtually
  fat-free fromage frais
10 g/1 tablespoon grated
  Parmesan cheese
sea salt, black pepper and
  freshly grated nutmeg,
  to season
8 slices wholemeal/
  whole-wheat toast,
  to serve

4 ramekins, lightly greased

serves 4

Put the kettle on to boil and preheat the oven to 180°C (350°F) Gas 4.

Cook the spinach in a covered pan until wilted, stirring once or twice. Drain off any excess liquid and season with nutmeg, salt and pepper to taste.

Divide the spinach between the prepared ramekins. Make a hollow in the spinach and break an egg into each one. Season lightly, then top each egg with a spoonful of fromage frais and a sprinkling of Parmesan cheese.

Put the ramekins in the roasting pan and pour boiling water around them to come halfway up the sides.

Bake in the preheated oven for 14–16 minutes, depending on how soft you like the yolks. Bear in mind that the eggs will carry on cooking after they have come out of the oven.

Serve immediately with two slices of toast per serving.

These baked eggs cooked 'en cocotte' or 'in a ramekin' transform just four ingredients into something truly sophisticated. Voilà! – a petit pot of deliciousness which is perfect for a quick brunch, lunch or hastily put together supper. Bon appétit!

eggs 'en cocotte'

60 g/1 cup fresh spinach,
  chopped
4 eggs
4 tablespoons whole milk
75 g/1 cup grated
  Parmesan cheese
sea salt and black pepper,
  to season

4 ramekins, buttered

serves 4

Preheat the oven to 200°C (400°F) Gas 6. Divide the spinach between the prepared ramekins. Crack an egg on top, add a spoonful of milk to each, then season and top with the Parmesan cheese.

Arrange the ramekins on a baking sheet in the preheated oven and cook for 6 minutes.

It's amazing how just three eggs can transform a stale loaf into a delicious breakfast pudding. Any dried fruit can be used, alone or in combination, as can different breads. Fresh fruit is also nice; diced apple is ideal (as is pear), pitted/stoned cherries, strawberries and even rhubarb, though you may need to increase the sugar quantity.

breakfast bread & butter pudding with dried apricots & cranberries

500 ml/2 cups whole milk (you may need a little more if your bread is thickly sliced)

2 tablespoons caster/ granulated sugar

3 eggs

¼ teaspoon ground cinnamon

8 slices wholemeal/ whole-wheat bread, torn into bite-size pieces

170 g/1 cup dried apricots, chopped

4 tablespoons dried cranberries (unsweetened)

honey or maple syrup, for drizzling

a baking dish, generously greased with butter

serves 4

Preheat the oven to 180°C (350°F) Gas 4.

Combine the milk, sugar, eggs and cinnamon in a bowl, and whisk well to blend. Set aside.

Put the dried apricot pieces and cranberries in a mixing bowl and stir to mix together.

Arrange half of the bread pieces in the prepared baking dish and sprinkle with half of the apricot mixture. Top with the remaining bread and the remaining apricot mixture and pour over the milk mixture.

Bake in the preheated oven for 35–45 minutes, until puffed, golden and just slightly wobbly in the middle.

Serve warm, with honey or maple syrup to drizzle over.

This Turkish egg dish is packed with so much flavour that you will be hooked from the first taste. Warmth from the cumin and dried chilli/hot red pepper flakes is mellowed by the yogurt and comes together with the pop of a poached egg. Pita or sliced sourdough also works well.

poached eggs on spinach with yogurt & spiced butter

1 small garlic clove, crushed
200 g/1 cup Greek yoghurt
50 g/3½ tablespoons butter
½ teaspoon cumin seeds
½ teaspoon dried chilli/hot red pepper flakes
½ teaspoon sea salt flakes
1 loaf Turkish flat bread, cut into 4 squares and halved horizontally
1 tablespoon olive oil
400 g/8 cups spinach
8 large eggs
sea salt and black pepper, to season

serves 4

Preheat the grill/broiler to high. Get everything ready before you start cooking: mix the garlic and yogurt. Put the butter, cumin, dried chilli/hot red pepper flakes and sea salt flakes in a small saucepan. Put the flat bread on a baking sheet. Fill two deep frying pans/skillets with water and bring to a boil over high heat.

Heat a wok, then add the oil and when hot, add the spinach in batches. Toss around the wok so it cooks evenly and when it is just wilted, take it off the heat, season and cover.

Reduce the heat under the frying pans/skillets to low so the water is barely simmering and break 4 eggs, far apart, into each one. Leave for 3 minutes.

Grill/broil the bread, cut-side up, until lightly toasted, then transfer to serving plates. Spread some garlic yogurt over the bread and heap a mound of spinach on top. Using a slotted spoon, sit a poached egg on top of each square of yogurty bread. Quickly heat the spiced butter until bubbling, pour over the eggs and serve.

Chicory is a sometimes underrated vegetable, unlike in France and Italy where they use it a lot, and not just in the salad bowl. It is so different when cooked, becoming silky smooth and slightly bitter, which is why it works so well against a sweet, smoky ham like Black Forest ham. The chilli/chile and lemon in the dressing wake up all the flavours, while the oozing yolk of a poached egg brings everything together.

caramelized chicory with Black Forest ham & poached eggs

25 g/1½ tablespoons butter
4 chicory heads, halved lengthways
4 eggs
100 g/2 cups rocket/arugula
8 slices Black Forest ham
25 g/2 tablespoons shaved Parmesan cheese
sea salt and black pepper, to season

dressing
1 small garlic clove, finely chopped
1 fresh red chilli/chile, finely chopped
1 tablespoon red wine vinegar
2 tablespoons extra virgin olive oil
finely grated zest and juice of ½ lemon

serves 4

Preheat the oven to 140°C (275°F) Gas 1.

To make the dressing, put the garlic, chilli/chile and vinegar in a bowl and whisk in the olive oil and lemon zest and juice.

Heat the butter in a large frying pan/skillet over low heat and add the chicory, cut-side down. Season with salt and pepper, cover with a lid and leave the chicory to cook gently for 5–6 minutes. Remove the lid, turn up the heat and continue to cook for 5 minutes, until the chicory is golden. Turn the chicory halves over and cook for 3–4 minutes so the other side gets a chance to caramelize. Transfer to the preheated oven to keep warm.

Fill a large, deep frying pan/skillet with water and bring to a demure simmer. Crack the eggs around the edge so they don't touch and poach for exactly 3 minutes. Remove from the pan with a slotted spoon.

Place a little mound of rocket/arugula on each plate, top with two chicory halves and drape a slice of the Black Forest ham on top of each one. Place a poached egg on top of the ham. Scatter some Parmesan shavings around the plate and finish with a drizzle of the dressing.

These wraps are a cross between a crêpe and an omelette. You can use any smoked fish for this – salmon, mackerel and eel would all work just as well as the haddock used here. Make sure the avocado is soft and ripe and season it really well for best results.

smoked haddock, radish & avocado omelette wraps

6 eggs
2 tablespoons butter
200 g/7 oz. hot smoked haddock, flaked
50 g/1 cup watercress
1 ripe avocado, peeled, stoned/pitted and chopped
6 radishes, thinly sliced
2 tablespoons extra virgin olive oil
2 tablespoons freshly squeezed lemon juice
sea salt and black pepper, to season

serves 1

Preheat the oven to 140°C (275°F) Gas 1.

Gently beat the eggs in a bowl and season with salt and pepper. Put an ovenproof plate in the preheated oven to heat up.

Heat about 1 teaspoon of the butter in the frying pan/skillet over high heat and swirl it around the pan. Pour in about 3 tablespoons of the beaten eggs – just enough to coat the base of the pan.

Wait for 30 seconds, then flip over. Repeat with the remaining mixture, using the same amount of butter each time, until you have about eight omelettes, keeping them warm on the plate in the preheated oven.

Meanwhile, put the smoked haddock, watercress, avocado and radishes in a large mixing bowl. Stir in the oil and lemon juice and season with pepper.

Lay two omelette wraps out on a board and spoon some of the haddock filling down the middle of each one, then roll up and transfer to a plate. Repeat with the remaining wraps and serve.

This is a dish built for lazy weekends spent with family and friends looking to fuel up before a long walk, or even cure a hangover. Fritters hold their own both on a breakfast table and later on if someone fires up a barbecue. Served with squashed roast tomatoes and prosciutto, and a dipping sauce of yogurt muddled with basil and mint or an avocado purée, this is indulgence at its finest. They also freeze well and can be happily warmed in the oven if you prefer to make a big batch ready to whip out and impress guests.

pea, basil & feta fritters with roast tomatoes

200 g/1⅓ cups frozen peas, quickly defrosted (you can use the pan you'll fry the fritters in)
100 g/¾ cup plain/all-purpose flour
1 teaspoon baking powder
1 egg
150 ml/⅔ cup whole milk
grated zest of ½ lemon
100 g/⅔ cup crumbled feta cheese
30 fresh basil leaves, torn into small shreds
2 tablespoons olive oil
sea salt and black pepper, to season
100 g/3½ oz. prosciutto, to serve

roast tomatoes
300 g/2 cups cherry tomatoes, halved
2 tablespoons olive oil
2 tablespoons balsamic vinegar

serves 4

Preheat the oven to 180°C (350°F) Gas 4.

For the roast tomatoes, put the halved cherry tomatoes on a baking sheet, drizzle with the olive oil and vinegar and sprinkle with a few pinches of salt. Roast in the preheated oven for 25–35 minutes until the tomatoes are lightly caramelized. Turn the oven off.

For the fritters, lightly defrost the peas over medium heat in a saucepan. Combine the flour, baking powder, egg, milk and lemon zest in a mixing bowl. Stir in the crumbled feta, torn basil and defrosted peas. Season well.

Heat 1 tablespoon of the olive oil in the frying pan/skillet. Spoon 1½ tablespoons of batter per fritter into the hot pan. Cook the fritters in batches over medium heat until you see small holes appearing on the surface. Gently flip with a spatula and cook for 2 minutes on the other side. Transfer to the still-warm oven while you make the rest.

Serve the fritters with the roast tomatoes and prosciutto.

cook's note
Substitute mint or parsley for the basil here, and goat's cheese, torn mozzarella or halloumi for the feta.

Corn fritters are a menu staple in nearly every café in Australia and New Zealand. No two recipes are ever the same as everyone has their own opinion on what makes the perfect fritter. Be brave and tweak this recipe to your own tastes.

corn fritters with roast tomatoes & smashed avocado

1 courgette/zucchini, grated
400 g/2½ cups cherry vine tomatoes
olive oil, to drizzle
4 eggs
180 g/1⅓ cups self-raising/rising flour
50 g/1¾ oz. Parmesan cheese, grated
100 ml/scant ½ cup buttermilk
1 teaspoon paprika
½ teaspoon cayenne pepper
1 tablespoon chopped coriander/cilantro
fresh corn kernels cut from 2–3 cobs
sunflower oil, for frying
sea salt and black pepper, to season

smashed avocado

3 avocados
freshly squeezed juice of 2 limes and the grated zest of 1
¼ red onion, finely diced
1 teaspoon hot sauce

to serve

fresh spinach
crème fraîche (or sour cream)

serves 6

Put the grated courgette/zucchini into a colander set over a large mixing bowl. Sprinkle with ½ teaspoon of salt and leave for 30 minutes–1 hour so it releases its moisture. Squeeze the grated courgette/zucchini with your hands to get rid of as much moisture as possible and set aside.

For the roast tomatoes, preheat the oven to 180°C (350°F) Gas 4. Arrange the tomatoes on a baking sheet, drizzle with olive oil and season with salt and pepper. Roast in the preheated oven for 15–20 minutes, or until the skins begin to split.

Reduce the oven temperature to 170°C (325°F) Gas 3 and prepare the fritter batter.

In a large, clean, dry mixing bowl, lightly whisk the eggs. Add in the flour, grated Parmesan cheese, buttermilk, paprika, cayenne pepper, ½ teaspoon of salt, a pinch of pepper and chopped coriander/cilantro. Stir in the squeezed courgette/zucchini and corn kernels, ensuring the vegetables are evenly coated in batter.

Add enough sunflower oil to thinly cover the bottom of a heavy-bottomed frying pan/skillet and set over medium heat.

Ladle generous spoonfuls of batter into the pan and cook for about 4 minutes on each side, until golden brown. Transfer to a clean baking sheet and put in the still-warm oven for 4–5 minutes to ensure they are cooked through. Cook the remaining batter in the same way, adding a little more oil to the pan each time, if required.

Just before serving, roughly mash the avocados with a fork, leaving them fairly chunky. Stir in the lime juice and zest, onion and hot sauce. Season generously with salt and serve with the fritters, roast tomatoes, a handful of fresh spinach and a dollop of crème fraîche.

These gluten-free muffins are quick and simple to prepare, and are deliciously light and tasty. Needing only a few ingredients, they are a great standby recipe. To make them dairy-free, omit the cheese and replace with some corn kernels instead.

cheese & onion soufflé muffins

1 onion, finely chopped
1 tablespoon sunflower oil
5 eggs, separated
125 g/1¼ cups grated Red Leicester or mature/sharp Cheddar cheese
sea salt and black pepper, to season

a 12-hole muffin pan, well greased

makes 12

Preheat the oven to 180°C (350°F) Gas 4.

In a frying pan/skillet set over medium heat, cook the onion in the oil until softened and lightly golden brown, then leave to cool.

In a mixing bowl, stir together the egg yolks, cooked onion and grated cheese, and season well.

Put the egg whites in a separate bowl and whisk them to stiff peaks.

Gently fold the egg whites into the cheese mixture with a spatula until the cheese and onions are evenly distributed through the egg but without knocking out too much air. Spoon the mixture into the holes of the muffin pan and bake in the preheated oven for 20–25 minutes until the soufflés have risen and are golden brown. Remove the muffins from the pan while still warm. These muffins are best served straight away.

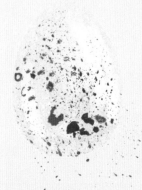

appetizers

This is a take on traditional Scotch eggs for a little canapé. It's a very easy, no-fuss option to prepare, too.

'Scotch eggs'

12 quail eggs
6 slices prosciutto, coppa or Serrano ham
sea salt and black pepper, to season

makes 12

Hard-boil/cook the quail's eggs in a pan of boiling water for 5 minutes. Drain and plunge the eggs into cold water, then drain again and let cool. Remove the shells, dry the eggs with paper towels and then roll them in salt and pepper.

Cut each slice of cured ham lengthways down the middle (kitchen scissors are best for this) to make 12 half-slices in total.

Roll each shelled quail's egg up inside a half-slice of ham. You might need to insert a cocktail stick/toothpick through each canapé if the quail eggs are bigger, but they'll hold together by themselves if they're small.

Serve immediately.

Dukkha is an Egyptian dry spice blend that has a multitude of uses – as a salad sprinkle, a seasoning on lamb chops or a dip with bread and olive oil. Best of all, serve it as a snack with hard-boiled/cooked eggs.

dukkha eggs (pictured, page 2)

100 g/¾ cup hazelnuts
20 g/¼ cup pistachios
15 g/2 tablespoons coriander seeds
1 tablespoon cumin seeds
40 g/5 tablespoons sesame seeds
2 teaspoons white or black peppercorns
½ teaspoon dried chilli/hot red pepper flakes
½ teaspoon sea salt
8–10 hard-boiled/cooked eggs (see page 10), to serve

makes 8–10

Preheat the oven to 170°C (325°F) Gas 3.

Scatter the hazelnuts and pistachios on separate baking sheets and roast in the preheated oven for 10 minutes. Remove from the oven and immediately wrap the hazelnuts in a clean kitchen cloth. Set aside to allow the steam to build for a minute before rubbing them within the kitchen towel to remove the loose skins. When both the pistachios and hazelnuts are cool, roughly crush them in a pestle and mortar to a chunky texture. Transfer to a large mixing bowl and set aside.

Put the coriander and cumin seeds in a preheated frying pan/skillet set over medium heat. Dry fry the seeds for a couple of minutes, shaking the pan from time to time, until they start to pop. Remove the seeds from the pan and crush in a pestle and mortar. Add to the nuts in the mixing bowl.

Put the sesame seeds in the same, dry pan and toast until lightly golden, giving the pan a shake every 30 seconds. Remove from the pan and grind in the pestle and mortar. Add to the nut and seed mixture.

Repeat this process with the white or black peppercorns.

Lightly grind the dried chilli/hot red pepper flakes in the pestle and mortar and add to the nut and seed mixture.

Finally, add the salt and mix everything together. The dukkha is now ready.

Peel the eggs and dip the tops in the dukkha to serve.

The term 'devilled' was first used to describe the act of adding spice to a dish, but devilled eggs are more than just spiced eggs. The yolk of a hard-boiled/cooked egg is carefully removed, mixed with mayonnaise and spices and returned to the hole of the white to serve. It's really quite a dainty affair with a devilish surprise on the tongue.

devilled eggs (pictured)

12 hard-boiled/cooked eggs (see page 10), peeled
4 tablespoons mayonnaise
1–2 tablespoons chilli/chili shrimp paste
sea salt and ground white pepper, to season
2 spring onions/scallions, sliced and 1 teaspoon black sesame seeds, to serve

makes 24

Halve the eggs lengthways and remove the yolks. Put the yolks into a bowl and break them up with a fork.

Mix in the mayonnaise and chilli/chili shrimp paste to taste. Season well with salt and white pepper. When completely smooth, either spoon the mixture back into the egg whites or pipe in using a piping/pastry bag fitted with a star-shaped nozzle/tip, if you have one.

Sprinkle over the sliced spring onions/scallions and black sesame seeds and serve immediately.

Blinis are a superb way to transform an egg with a little flour and yeast to wow your guests with very little effort. You can make the batter a day ahead, then let it have its final rising 30 minutes before cooking. They freeze well, too, and can be warmed up on a baking sheet in the oven.

blinis with salmon & crème fraîche

50 g/⅓ cup buckwheat flour
50 g/½ cup strong plain/all-purpose white flour
1 teaspoon salt
125 ml/½ cup whole milk
75 ml/⅓ cup crème fraîche (or sour cream), plus extra to serve
7 g/¼ oz. fast-action dried yeast
1 large egg, separated
sunflower oil, for frying
smoked salmon and snipped chives, to serve

makes 20

Sift the flours and salt into a large mixing bowl. Heat the milk in a saucepan until hand-hot. Add the crème fraîche and yeast, and stir until smooth. Pour onto the flours with the egg yolk and stir well to blend. Cover and leave to rise for 1 hour.

Beat the egg white with an electric handheld whisk until soft peaks form.

Fold into the batter, cover and leave for 30 minutes. Preheat the oven to 140°C (275°F) Gas 1.

To make the blinis, heat a heavy-bottomed frying pan/skillet over medium heat. Grease with a paper towel dipped in oil. Drop in 2 tablespoons of the batter. After 30 seconds bubbles will appear on the surface. Flip the blini over and cook for 30 seconds on the other side. Keep warm in the oven while you cook the rest.

Serve with crème fraîche (or sour cream), smoked salmon, chives and black pepper.

Bite-size eggs are so much more fun than the full-size variety and quail eggs are packed with protein to keep you going all day. A nice way to serve them is to mix a little mustard with mayo and slice in half ready to dip in.

Scotch quail eggs

12 quail eggs
600 g/1 lb. 5 oz. good-quality pork sausages
1 tablespoon finely chopped fresh parsley
1 tablespoon finely chopped fresh thyme (optional)
1 hen's egg yolk, beaten, plus 1 whole hen's egg
1 tablespoon plain/all-purpose flour
4 tablespoons whole milk
75 g/1 cup fine breadcrumbs
sunflower oil, for frying
sea salt and black pepper, to season

makes 12

Bring a small saucepan of water to the boil and gently lower in the quail eggs. Boil for 100 seconds, then plunge the boiled eggs immediately into cold water to stop further cooking. Once cold, one at a time, roll each egg gently along a work surface with the flat of your palm until the shell is all cracked, then peel away the shell. Set the peeled eggs aside until needed.

Remove the skins from the sausages and discard. Put the sausage meat in a large mixing bowl with the parsley, thyme, if using, and hen's egg yolk. Season with salt and pepper and stir to combine. Divide the mixture into 12 equal portions.

Put the plain/all-purpose flour seasoned with salt and pepper, the whole hen's egg beaten with milk, and the breadcrumbs each in separate shallow bowls.

Take a portion of sausage meat and make a patty with it in your palm. Place a peeled quail egg in the centre and gently mould the sausage meat around it before rolling it into a ball between your palms. Repeat with the rest of the sausage meat and quail eggs. Roll each Scotch egg firstly in the seasoned flour, then dip it in the egg wash before coating it in the breadcrumbs.

Pour the oil into a saucepan and bring up to smoking-hot temperature, around 180°C (350°F). Fry a few eggs at a time for about 4 minutes until they are golden brown all over.

Transfer to a plate lined with paper towels to soak up any excess oil and leave to cool before serving.

These fried patties should be packed with herbs – the more the merrier – especially the mint. They are versatile, so you can also use grated raw carrot or fried leeks if you choose. Once cooked, they keep well and can be enjoyed cold as well as hot, straight out of the pan.

courgette/zucchini, feta & herb patties

3 eggs
3 tablespoons plain/all-purpose flour
2 firm courgettes/zucchini
1 red or white onion, cut in half lengthways, in half again crossways, and sliced with the grain
200 g/7 oz. feta cheese, crumbled
1–2 fresh red or green chillies/chiles, deseeded and finely chopped
2 teaspoons dried mint
a bunch of fresh flat-leaf parsley, coarsely chopped
a bunch of fresh dill fronds, coarsely chopped
a big bunch of fresh mint leaves, coarsely chopped (reserve a little for garnishing)
sunflower oil, for frying
sea salt and black pepper, to season
1–2 lemons, cut into wedges, to serve

makes 6

In a big bowl, beat the eggs with the flour until smooth.

Trim off the ends of the courgettes/zucchini, but don't peel them. Grate the courgette/zucchini on the widest teeth of the grater, then squeeze out all of the water with your hands. Pile the courgette/zucchini on top of the flour and egg mixture.

Add the onion, feta, chillies/chiles, dried mint and fresh herbs and mix well with a large spoon or your hands. Season the mixture well with salt and pepper and set aside.

Heat a little sunflower oil in a heavy-based frying pan/skillet over medium heat – don't put in too much oil; you can always add more as you fry the patties.

Put 2–3 spoonfuls of the courgette/zucchini mixture into the pan and fry for about 2 minutes each side, pressing the patties down a little with a spatula, so that they are flat but quite thick, lightly browned and firm. Cook the patties in batches, adding more oil to the pan when necessary. Drain on paper towels and keep warm under foil, or in a warm oven.

Arrange the patties on a serving dish, garnish with the reserved mint, and serve with wedges of lemon to squeeze over them.

This is not technically a pâté, but a country terrine with a hidden egg in the centre. This recipe needs to be made the day before serving so that it has enough time to rest in the fridge ready for slicing.

pâté de campagne

30 g/2 tablespoons butter
2 tablespoons brandy
4 shallots, finely chopped
1 garlic clove, finely chopped
1 egg
4 tablespoons double/heavy cream
½ teaspoon Dijon mustard
a pinch of fresh thyme leaves
400 g/14 oz. pork loin or shoulder (as much fat removed as possible), trimmed and cut into 1-cm/½-inch dice
6 slices prosciutto
100 g/3½ oz. ham hock, chopped (optional)
1 hard-boiled/cooked egg (see page 10), peeled
sea salt and black pepper, to season
oatcakes or toasted baguette slices, to serve

a 20 x 10-cm/8 x 4-inch loaf pan, greased

serves 1

Preheat the oven to 180°C (350°F) Gas 4.

Melt the butter in a frying pan/skillet over medium heat, then add the brandy. Let it boil and reduce for a minute, then add the shallots and garlic. Once those have softened, remove the pan from the heat and let cool.

In a bowl, beat the egg and then stir in the cream, mustard and thyme, and season with salt and pepper. Add the diced pork, then stir in the cooled shallot mixture and any juices from the pan.

Lay the slices of prosciutto across the bottom and up the sides of the prepared loaf pan so that they line the pan. I recommend leaving just a small gap between the slices so that the loaf is easier to slice once it's cooked and then chilled. Spoon half of the pork mixture into the pan and then sprinkle the ham hock pieces across the middle, if using. Place a peeled hard-boiled/cooked egg in the middle.

Spoon the remaining pork mixture on top and then fold in the ends of the prosciutto, if the slices are longer than the inside surface of the loaf pan.

Cover the pan tightly with foil.

Take a larger roasting dish and put 2.5 cm/1 inch of water in the bottom. Lower the loaf pan into the water and cook in the preheated oven for 1 hour, until the mixture around the meat has thickened and the meat is firm to the touch. Remove the loaf pan from the water bath and let cool for 30 minutes.

The loaf pan should now be cool enough to move to the fridge to finish setting. The pâté will take a good few hours to set properly, and it is recommended to make it a day ahead.

Let it come to room temperature for about 20–30 minutes before serving. Run a knife around the edge of the loaf to release it from the sides of the pan and then turn it out onto a board. Serve with oatcakes or toasted baguette slices.

This pâté is heavenly served with an ice-cold glass of dry white wine like Sancerre and maybe a game of pétanque in a French courtyard!

These little egg-filled pasties are quite filling, and because they're mildly flavoured, they work well with simple soups. They are also good for serving at parties with a cold beer or cocktail. Suitable for freezing, you will always have a quick snack to hand. Simply defrost and reheat in the oven until piping hot before serving.

egg-rice pockets

200 g/1½ cups strong white bread flour
200 g/1 stick plus 5½ tablespoons butter, chilled and cubed
75 ml/⅓ cup very cold water

filling
100 g/½ cup short-grain rice (pudding rice)
2 eggs, plus 1 extra, lightly beaten, for glazing
35 g/2¼ tablespoons butter, melted
sea salt and black pepper, to season

a round cookie cutter (or an upturned cup), about 10 cm/4 inch in diameter 1–2 baking sheets, lined with baking parchment

makes 12–16

Put the flour in a large mixing bowl. Add the cubed butter and rub in using your fingertips until the mixture resembles fine breadcrumbs.

Gradually add the very cold water to the flour mixture, stirring with a round-bladed knife until a dough forms. Bring the dough together to form a ball and wrap in clingfilm/plastic wrap. Set in the fridge to rest for at least for 2 hours, or overnight if possible.

To make the filling, cook the rice according to the manufacturer's instructions. When the rice is ready, it should be quite sticky. Set aside to cool while you make the rest of the filling.

Meanwhile, put the eggs in a small saucepan of cold water and bring to a gentle boil. Simmer for 6–7 minutes, until just hard. Transfer to a bowl of cold water and immerse until the eggs are cool enough to handle. Peel and chop them finely, then mix with the melted butter and cooked rice. Season with salt and pepper to taste. Set aside.

Preheat the oven to 220°C (425°F) Gas 7.

Take the pastry out of the fridge and remove the clingfilm/plastic wrap. Roll the pastry out on a lightly floured surface, with a rolling pin, until about 3-mm/⅛-inch thick. It may be quite sticky, so you might need to dust more flour on the work surface.

Use the cookie cutter to cut out rounds from the pastry. Gather up the offcuts of pastry and refrigerate them briefly before rolling out and cutting out more rounds.

Drop a generous tablespoon of filling onto each pastry round. Fold in half to make a semi-circle and encase the filling. Using your fingers, pinch the edges together to seal the parcels. Arrange on the prepared baking sheets.

Brush the extra beaten egg over the parcels with a pastry brush, to glaze them, then prick the top of each one once with a fork. Bake in the preheated oven for about 15 minutes, or until golden brown. Serve hot or cold.

A frittata is a baked Italian omelette that is delicious at any time of the day, served hot or cold. It makes a great canapé – cut into small bite-size squares which can be picked up with a cocktail stick/toothpick.

chorizo frittata bites (pictured)

4 x 60-g/2-oz. chorizo
16 eggs
300 ml/1¼ cups crème fraîche (or sour cream)
a pinch each of sea salt and black pepper
1 tablespoon olive oil
1 red onion, finely chopped
1 garlic clove, crushed
130 g/1 cup fresh or frozen peas
1 red (bell) pepper, deseeded and cut into strips
60 g/1¼ cups baby spinach
mayonnaise (see page 124), to serve

serves 8–10

Preheat the oven to 180°C (350°F) Gas 4.

Put the chorizo on a baking sheet and cook in the preheated oven for 12 minutes. Remove from the oven, drain on paper towels and cut into 1-cm/⅜-inch slices. Cover and set aside. Reduce the oven temperature to 110°C (225°F) Gas ¼.

Break the eggs into a large mixing bowl with the crème fraîche and lightly whisk. Season with the salt and pepper and set aside. Heat the oil in a large ovenproof frying pan/skillet set over low–medium heat. Add the onion and garlic, and sauté until soft but not coloured. Add the sliced chorizo, peas and (bell) pepper strips, and cook for 2–3 minutes, stirring occasionally. Add the baby spinach and stir until it just begins to wilt.

Arrange the mix evenly over the base of the pan and carefully pour in the egg mixture. Reduce the heat and gently cook the frittata, moving the egg in a little from the edge of the pan as it cooks. After about 10 minutes, once it has just set on the bottom and the sides, place the pan in the oven for 15–20 minutes, until the frittata is lightly golden and just set in the middle. Remove from the oven and set aside to cool.

Turn out the frittata, cut into 4-cm/1½-inch squares and serve.

mini vegetable frittatas

whites of 4 spring onions/scallions, thinly sliced
3 courgettes/zucchini, quartered lengthways
1 red (bell) pepper, diced
2 tablespoons olive oil
a pinch of dried oregano
100 g/1½ cups sun-dried tomatoes
125 g/4½ oz. Gruyère cheese
8 large eggs
125 ml/½ cup single/light cream
black pepper, to season

a 12-hole muffin pan, greased

makes 12

Preheat the oven to 180°C (350°F) Gas 4.

Put the sliced spring onions/scallions, courgettes/zucchini, and (bell) pepper into a frying pan/skillet with the olive oil and oregano. Set over medium heat and cook for 5 minutes.

Cut the sun-dried tomatoes into 1-cm/⅜-inch pieces but keep separate from the onion mixture. Cut the cheese into 1-cm/⅜-inch cubes and add to the tomatoes.

Break the eggs into a bowl. Pour in the cream, add several grinds of pepper then gently beat the eggs and cream together until thoroughly mixed.

Add all the other ingredients to the bowl and stir. Ladle the mixture into the prepred muffin pan and bake in the preheated oven for 25 minutes.

Remove from the oven, lift from the pan with an off-set palette knife and serve warm.

This is a wonderfully warming and comforting dish – a version of 'chile con huevo' – long associated with the long, hot days and even longer, frosty nights of the vast flat plains of the Texas Panhandle. It originated in the Mexican border country but is now fairly common throughout the United States. Although this recipe is often cooked in a single casserole dish, in this version the mixture is divided into individual ramekins before the eggs are added, and served as an appetizer.

baked chilli/chile eggs

25 g/2 tablespoons butter
1 garlic clove, crushed
125 g/4 oz. smoked ham, chopped
225 g/8 oz. mushrooms, diced
2 fresh hot green chillies/ chiles, finely chopped
225 ml/1 cup sour cream
2 teaspoons dried parsley
½ teaspoon dried oregano
6 eggs
200 g/2 cups grated mature Cheddar cheese
sea salt and black pepper, to season

to serve
toast, rubbed with a garlic clove
hot sauce

6 ramekins

serves 6

Preheat the oven to 190°C (375°F) Gas 5.

Melt the butter in a heavy-based frying pan/skillet over medium heat and fry the garlic and ham for about 2 minutes, stirring regularly to prevent the garlic from burning. Add the mushrooms and chillies/chiles and continue to cook for about 5–10 minutes until the mushrooms start to brown and the chillies begin to soften. Remove from the heat and stir in the sour cream, parsley and oregano. Season lightly with salt and pepper. Divide the mixture equally between the ramekins and let stand for about 10 minutes to allow the flavours to blend together.

Make a shallow hollow in each mixture and carefully break an egg in. Season the eggs with salt and pepper.

Bake in the preheated oven for 20–25 minutes or until the egg whites have set. Remove the ramekins from the oven and sprinkle the grated cheese over all of them. Return to the oven for about 5 minutes, or until the cheese is bubbling. Serve immediately with garlicky toast and a bottle of hot sauce to splash on the eggs.

cook's notes:
• If it is very warm in your kitchen, put the mixture in the fridge to set a little before making the hollows and adding the eggs.
• For an even more luxurious (and meat-free) alternative, substitute the smoked ham for smoked salmon. Serve with a lightly dressed baby leaf salad.

A steak tartare carts the best bits of a burger – the grunt of meat, the lick of ketchup and the salty punch of pickle – but with the run of an egg yolk to mix everything together. Smaller mounds of tartare pair well with quail egg yolks for a daintier dish. The mustard and cheese toasts are the perfect sidekick.

steak tartare with mustard cheese toasts

3 tablespoons tomato ketchup
1 tablespoon Dijon mustard
3 teaspoons Worcestershire sauce
a generous splash of Tabasco sauce
1 tablespoon olive oil, plus extra for drizzling
500 g/1 lb. 2 oz. fillet of beef, finely chopped
1½ tablespoons chopped gherkins
3 tablespoons finely chopped fresh flat-leaf parsley
1½ tablespoons chopped capers
1½ tablespoons finely chopped shallot
4 egg yolks
sea salt and black pepper, to season
hot sourdough toast or Mustard Cheese Toasts (below), to serve

mustard cheese toasts
(optional)
2 tablespoons butter, melted
1 tablespoon hot English mustard
75 g/¾ cup grated Cheddar cheese
1 baguette, sliced into 1-cm/½-inch slices

serves 4

If making the mustard cheese toasts, combine the melted butter and English mustard and brush the mixture over the slices of baguette. Top with cheese and grill/broil under medium heat for 5 minutes, until the tops are melted and bubbly.

Meanwhile, put the tomato ketchup, Dijon mustard, Worcestershire sauce, Tabasco sauce and olive oil in a large mixing bowl and whisk to combine. Add all the other ingredients except the egg yolks and mix well – the finely chopped beef fillet should be speckled with the other ingredients.

Divide the mixture between chilled plates – you could fill metal rings or round cookie cutters to form perfect circles – and make a well in the top of each round in the middle to sit the whole egg yolk into.

Put the egg yolks in the wells.

Lightly drizzle the plate with olive oil, and season with salt and pepper. Serve immediately with hot sourdough toast (as pictured) or the mustard cheese toasts.

Full of roast new potatoes, topped off with a cheesy egg mixture, these simple little tartlets make an excellent addition to a platter of mini dishes. Serve them alongside some of the other appetizers in this book at a dinner party.

roast potato & spring onion/ scallion tartlets

500 g/1 lb. 2 oz. baby new
  potatoes, halved
40 ml/4 tablespoons olive
  oil
1½ teaspoons salt
½ teaspoon black pepper
5 spring onions/scallions,
  sliced
2 garlic cloves, crushed
70 g/¾ cup grated mature
  Cheddar cheese
170 ml/¾ cup double/
  heavy cream
1 large egg

spelt dough
200 g/1⅔ cups spelt flour
1 teaspoon fast-action
  dried yeast
½ teaspoon salt
2 tablespoons olive oil
1 egg
60 ml/¼ cup warm water

6 x 10-cm/4-inch loose-based fluted tartlet pans, greased

makes 6

To make the spelt dough, mix the flour, yeast and salt in a bowl. Make a well in the centre and pour in the oil, egg and warm water. Draw everything together with your hands to form a soft dough.

Transfer the dough to a lightly floured surface and knead for 2–3 minutes. The dough should be soft but not sticky. If it is sticky, add a little flour and knead again. Roll out the dough with a rolling pin until 3-mm/⅛-inch thick. Line the tartlet pans with the dough but do not trim the edges yet.

Preheat the oven to 200°C (400°F) Gas 6.

Put the potatoes, oil, salt and pepper in a roasting pan and toss until evenly coated. Cover the pan with foil and roast in the preheated oven for 20 minutes. Remove from the oven and leave to cool for about 10 minutes.

Reduce the oven temperature to 170°C (325°F) Gas 3.

Stir the spring onions/scallions, garlic and cheese into the roast potatoes and mix well.

Mix together the cream and egg in a bowl, then divide half between the tartlet shells. Spread the vegetables over the top, then pour in the remaining cream mixture. Now trim the excess dough neatly around the edges.

Bake in the oven for 25 minutes, or until the filling looks golden. Remove from the oven and leave to cool for 5 minutes, then serve warm.

main meals

Bulgogi is a Korean dish of shredded beef, fresh vegetables and sometimes rice. The beef is marinated in a potent sweet and sharp sauce before being grilled on a very hot barbecue. In Korea, barbecue restaurants abound, and each one usually specialises in just one dish: red pork, short rib or beef bulgogi. Each table has its own individual grill where either the customers or waiter cook the marinated meat quickly to order. Served with lots of fresh salad ingredients and usually some form of pickle, you can create your own perfect balance of flavours. An egg is more commonly served with bibimbap (see page 111), but it works wonderfully well here to bring the textures and flavours together in each forkful.

bulgogi salad

400 g/14 oz. rib-eye steak, thinly sliced (partially freezing the beef will help you cut clean slices)
½ onion, sliced into very thin half moons
4 eggs
1 Asian pear, cored and cut into thin slivers
¼ iceberg lettuce, finely shredded
¼ white cabbage, finely shredded
hot sauce, to serve

beef marinade
3 tablespoons soy sauce
2 tablespoons caster/ granulated sugar
½ tablespoon sesame oil
3 garlic cloves, finely chopped
1 tablespoon toasted sesame seeds
a pinch of chilli powder
1 teaspoon black pepper
a 5-cm/2-inch piece of fresh ginger, grated

serves 4

Whisk together the ingredients for the beef marinade. Add the steak and onion slices and massage to combine. Cover and set in the fridge for 1 hour.

Heat a barbecue or frying pan/ skillet over high heat and grill or pan-fry the steak and onions in single layers until the edges are crisp. Discard any leftover marinade.

Fry the eggs following the instructions on page 11, keeping the yolks runny.

Combine the nashi pear, lettuce and cabbage and divide between bowls. Top with the beef, onion and fried egg. Serve with hot sauce.

Served in a steaming hot stone bowl, the presentation of this guilt-free dish is just as exciting as the punchy chilli/chile and sesame flavours inside. The fried (or sometimes raw) egg nestled amongst the other ingredients makes this dish sing. Good-quality ingredients make a world of difference for a truly authentic Korean taste, and gochujang, which is a slightly sweet but fiery chilli/chile paste, is well worth seeking out in Asian food stores.

bibimbap

400 g/14 oz. pork belly, chopped into thin 2.5-cm/1-inch pieces
400 g/2 cups short-grain brown rice (or brown sushi rice)
vegetable (or sunflower or rapeseed) oil, for frying
2 carrots, cut into thin strips
½ teaspoon toasted sesame oil
½ teaspoon dark soy sauce
½ teaspoon agave syrup
150 g/5 oz. oyster (or shiitake) mushrooms
150 g/5½ oz. beansprouts
3 onions, sliced
200 g/7 oz. spinach
4 eggs
2 spring onions/scallions, finely chopped
sea salt and black pepper, to season
black sesame seeds, to serve

gochujang sauce
4 tablespoons gochujang paste
4 tablespoons toasted sesame oil
4 tablespoons dark soy sauce
2 garlic cloves, crushed
2 tablespoons agave syrup

serves 4

To make the gochujang sauce, mix together all the ingredients. Pour half the sauce over the pork belly in a bowl, cover and marinate in the fridge for at least 1 hour. Cook the rice according to the packet instructions and keep warm.

While the rice is cooking, heat 1 tablespoon of oil in a frying pan/skillet or wok and stir-fry the carrots until beginning to soften. Add the sesame oil, soy sauce and agave syrup. Cook for 1 minute over high heat, then set aside on a plate. Cook the mushrooms, beansprouts, onions and spinach (which will wilt down) separately in the same pan/skillet, and in the same way, seasoning with salt and pepper at the end. It is normal for the vegetables to be served at room temperature, as long as the rice, meat and eggs are hot, so don't worry about keeping them warm.

Next, stir-fry the marinated pork (with the sauce it was sitting in) until cooked through. The sauce should reduce down a little with the heat, intensifying all the flavours.

In a separate frying pan/skillet, fry the eggs however you like them (see page 11) – it is nice to have the yolk a little soft for this dish.

Dish the hot rice into bowls and top with individual piles of vegetables and meat, finishing off with the egg in the middle and a sprinkling of spring onions/scallions and sesame seeds.

Serve with the gochujang sauce, adding as much or as little as you like. The Korean way of eating this is to mix the whole thing together like crazy until all the ingredients are combined. If it is not punchy enough, add more sauce.

The Nice salad is a classic. It evokes memories of a warm breeze coming off the Mediterranean and sand in between the toes – the perfect tonic for a hot day. The colours, vibrant and rich, complement the simple flavours that harmonize perfectly in this dish. In Provence they sometimes use artichokes instead of potatoes, so if you're cutting your carbs, this is a great alternative.

salade Niçoise with roast vine tomatoes

10 new potatoes, boiled and halved

225 g/8 oz.green beans, trimmed

325 g/11½ oz. vine tomatoes

75 g/½ cup Kalamata olives, stoned/ pitted

2 tablespoons extra virgin olive oil

5 eggs

1 lemon, halved

4 x 175-g/6-oz. tuna steaks (2.5-cm/1-inch thick)

4 little gem/Bibb lettuce, quartered lengthways

12 anchovies in olive oil

a large handful of fresh basil leaves (optional)

sea salt and black pepper, to season

French dressing

3 tablespoons white wine vinegar

4 tablespoons extra virgin olive oil

1 generous teaspoon Dijon mustard

1 garlic clove, crushed

serves 4–6

Preheat the oven to 200°C (400°F) Gas 6.

Put the new potatoes in a lidded saucepan (preferably with a steaming basket attachment) and bring to a boil. After 10 minutes add a steamer above the saucepan with the trimmed green beans in. Steam the beans for 4 minutes, then transfer them to a large roasting pan.

Add the tomatoes (still on the vine) and olives to the roasting pan and drizzle over the olive oil. Pop the pan in the preheated oven for 12–15 minutes.

Remove the potatoes from the boil (they should have had around 15 minutes total cooking time) and blanch in cold water to cool before draining and halving.

Boil the eggs for 6 minutes (see page 10), then put the pan under cold running water for a couple of minutes to cool down. When cool, peel the eggs and cut them in half.

Transfer the roast tomatoes, green beans, olives and any warm olive oil

to a dish to cool, squeeze over the juice of half a lemon and toss well.

Heat a ridged grill pan over medium–high heat for 5 minutes. Brush the tuna steaks with olive oil and season really well with salt and pepper before placing the steaks in the pan. Cook for 3–4 minutes on each side, until the tuna is cooked through.

Lay the lettuce leaves in a large container and scatter over the new potatoes and anchovies, then add the halved, boiled/cooked eggs, green beans, roasted tomatoes and olives. You can either choose to keep the tuna steaks whole and place them on the salad, or break them into flaky chunks and toss through. Transport the vinaigrette separately and drizzle it over the salad just before serving, otherwise the leaves can wilt a little. Sprinkle with fresh basil leaves, if using, also just before serving.

French dressing

To make the dressing, add a generous pinch of sea salt to the vinegar and mix to dissolve. Add the olive oil, Dijon mustard and garlic, and mix well before sprinkling over the salad.

With just four ingredients: eggs, cheese, crème fraîche and black pepper, you can rustle up a rich sauce to create a truly satisfying supper. The trick here is to add the hot cooked pasta to the beaten egg right before serving to limit its contact with the heat. Returning it to the pan for a moment or two is enough to cook the egg without it scrambling.

spaghetti carbonara

200 g/7 oz. dried spaghetti (or Fresh Egg Pasta, see page 116)

50 g/3½ tablespoons butter

2 garlic cloves, finely chopped

200 g/7 oz. pancetta or streaky/fatty bacon, cut into small cubes

2 eggs, beaten

75 g/scant ½ cup finely grated Parmesan cheese

a big pinch of fresh parsley, chopped

1 tablespoon crème fraîche (or sour cream)

sea salt and black pepper, to season

serves 2

First, cook the spaghetti in a saucepan of lightly salted boiling water until it is cooked to your liking. Once the spaghetti is cooked, drain it, reserving 5 mm/¼ inch of the cooking water in the base of the pan, and keep this over low heat.

Meanwhile, melt the butter in a frying pan/skillet over medium heat and fry the garlic until soft. Add the pancetta and fry until crispy and browned. Remove from the heat and keep warm in the pan.

In a large bowl, beat the eggs and then mix in most of the Parmesan cheese, reserving just a little cheese to sprinkle on the top. Add the parsley and crème fraîche and a good crunch of black pepper. Set aside.

Add the drained hot spaghetti to the beaten egg mixture and mix a little, then return the spaghetti and egg mixture to the pan containing the reserved pasta cooking water and stir. You don't want the egg mixture to scramble, but let it mix with the hot pasta water to create a sauce. Stir in the crispy pancetta and garlic mixture.

Serve immediately with the remaining Parmesan cheese sprinkled on top, and a crunch more pepper or a little freshly chopped parsley, as you wish.

Nothing beats homemade pasta – not even store-bought 'fresh'. The texture is silky, the cooked dough itself very light. These quantities are only guidelines – depending on humidity, type of flour used and so on, you may have to add more or less flour. As a guide, the dough must not be too soft – it should require some serious effort when kneading!

fresh egg pasta

**200 g/1½ cups plain/
all-purpose white flour
(or Italian '00' flour)
2 eggs
a pinch of sea salt
1 tablespoon olive oil**

flavoured pasta
(choose one of the following)
**150 g/5 oz. frozen leaf
spinach, cooked and
drained of moisture
2 tablespoons tomato
purée/paste
2 tablespoons grated
cooked beetroot/beet
1 sachet powdered
saffron mixed with
2 tablespoons hot water
3 tablespoons finely
chopped fresh green
herbs
1 sachet of squid ink**

a pasta machine (optional)

serves 2–4

To make the pasta the traditional way, sift the flour onto a clean work surface and make a well in the centre with your fist. Break the eggs into the well, add a pinch of salt and the oil. Gradually mix the eggs into the flour with the fingers of one hand, and bring it together into a firm dough. If the dough looks too dry, add a few drops of water, if too wet add more flour. Knead the pasta until smooth, lightly massage it with a hint of olive oil, pop into a polythene food bag and allow to rest for at least 30 minutes before rolling out. The pasta will be much more elastic after resting.

Roll the pasta dough out thinly on a lightly floured surface or roll out using a pasta machine. Roll or fold one end loosely towards the centre of the sheet, then do the same with the other so that they almost meet in the middle. Lift one folded side on top of the other – do not press down on the fold. Working quickly and deftly with one motion, cut into thin slices with a sharp knife, down the length of the folded pasta. Immediately unravel the slices to reveal the pasta ribbons – you can do this by inserting the back of a large knife and shaking them loose. Hang to dry a little before cooking or dust well with semolina flour and arrange in loose 'nests' on a basket or a baking sheet lined with a clean kitchen cloth.

flavoured pastas

Follow the basic recipe (see left) with the following additions:

spinach pasta Cook the spinach and squeeze out all the moisture. Blend with 1 egg until very smooth and season well with salt and pepper.

tomato pasta Add the tomato purée/paste to the well in the flour. Use 1 large egg instead of 2 medium ones.

beetroot/beet pasta Add the grated cooked beetroot/beet to the well in the flour. Use 1 large egg instead of 2 medium ones.

saffron pasta Soak a sachet/package of powdered saffron in 2 tablespoons hot water for 15 minutes. Use 1 large egg instead of 2 medium ones and whisk in the saffron water before adding to the flour.

herb pasta Add the fresh green herbs to the well in the flour.

squid ink pasta Add the squid ink to the eggs before adding to the flour.

A light-textured soufflé, presented straight from the oven, makes an elegant meal. Serve this with a crisp green side salad.

spinach & tomato soufflé

500 g/1 lb. 2 oz. fresh
  spinach
300 g/10 oz. ripe
  tomatoes
½ tablespoon olive oil
1 small onion, finely
  chopped
1 bay leaf
1 tablespoon tomato
  purée/paste
50 g/3 tablespoons butter
50 g/3½ tablespoons
  plain/all-purpose flour
200 ml/¾ cup warm
  whole milk
5 eggs, separated, plus
  1 egg white, whisked
sea salt, black pepper and
  freshly grated nutmeg,
  to season

*a 2-litre/quart capacity
  soufflé dish, greased*

serves 6

Preheat the oven to 200°C (400°F) Gas 6.

Rinse the spinach under cold, running water. Put it in a saucepan or pot, cover with boiling water and set over medium heat. Cook for 2–3 minutes until wilted, then drain, cool, squeeze dry and roughly chop.

Next, scald the tomatoes. Pour boiling water over the ripe tomatoes in a heatproof bowl. Set aside for 1 minute, drain and carefully peel off the skin using a sharp knife. Roughly chop, reserving any juices, and set aside.

Heat the oil in a frying pan/skillet set over medium heat. Add the onion and bay leaf and fry for 2 minutes, until softened. Add the chopped tomatoes and their juices, cover and cook for 5 minutes. Uncover, mix with a wooden spoon to help the tomatoes break down, stir in the tomato purée/paste and cook uncovered for 5 minutes to form a thick sauce. Remove and discard the bay leaf.

In a separate heavy-bottomed saucepan or pot set over a medium heat, melt the butter. Mix in the flour, stirring well. Gradually stir in the warm milk and cook, stirring continuously, until it thickens. Season with salt, pepper and nutmeg.

Remove the white sauce from heat. Mix in the tomato sauce, then the spinach. Check and adjust the seasoning if necessary. Beat in the egg yolks, one at a time, and set aside.

Whisk the egg whites until stiff peaks form. Stir a spoonful of the whisked egg white into the soufflé mixture to loosen it. Lightly and gently fold in the remaining whisked egg white. Pour into the prepared soufflé dish and bake in the preheated oven for 1 hour, until the soufflé has risen and turns golden brown. Serve at once.

A classic tart from Lorraine, in north-eastern France, and the forerunner of many copies. Made well and with the best ingredients, this simplest of dishes is food fit for the gods. Adding a little grated Gruyère cheese to the filling adds a heady depth of flavour.

quiche Lorraine

200 g/7 oz. bacon lardons (or cubed pancetta)
5 eggs
200 ml/¾ cup double/ heavy cream (or crème fraîche)
50 g/½ cup grated Gruyère cheese
sea salt, black pepper and freshly grated nutmeg, to season

shortcrust pastry

250 g/2 cups plain/all-purpose flour
a pinch of salt
50 g/3½ tablespoons lard, chilled and diced
75 g/5 tablespoons butter, chilled and diced
2–3 tablespoons chilled water

a 23-cm/9-inch diameter (or 20-cm/8-inch square) tart pan
baking beans

serves 4–6

To make the shortcrust pastry, sift the flour and the salt together in a bowl. Rub the lard and butter until the mixture resembles breadcrumbs. Add the water, mixing lightly with a knife to bring the pastry together. Knead for 2–3 minutes then shape into a ball. Wrap in clingfilm/plastic wrap and chill for 30 minutes before rolling. Bring the pastry to room temperature and preheat the oven to 200°C (400°F) Gas 6.

Roll out the pastry thinly on a lightly floured surface and use to line the tart pan. Prick the base, chill or freeze for 15 minutes, then line with foil and baking beans. Bake for 10–12 minutes, remove the beans and foil, and bake again for 5–7 minutes. To prevent the pastry from going soggy, brush with beaten egg and bake for 8–10 minutes.

Heat a frying pan/skillet and fry the bacon or pancetta until brown and crisp, then drain on paper towels. Scatter over the base of the pastry case.

Put the eggs and cream into a bowl, beat well, and season with salt, pepper and nutmeg to taste. Carefully pour the mixture over the bacon and sprinkle with the Gruyère cheese.

Bake for about 25 minutes until just set, golden brown and puffy.

Serve warm or at room temperature.

Matambre, or 'hunger killer', is a classic Argentinian dish that can be served as an appetizer, sliced and eaten in a bread roll or dished up with a potato salad as here for a hearty main meal. Rolled-up tender steak encases a potent stuffing of fresh herbs and olives and no less than six hard-boiled/cooked eggs.

matambre

a 900-g/2-lb. flank steak
6 leafy stalks red Swiss chard
30 g/⅓ cup grated Parmesan cheese
2 garlic cloves, finely chopped
60 g/½ cup Kalamata olives, stoned/pitted and roughly chopped
small bunches of fresh flat-leaf parsley, marjoram and oregano (leaves only), roughly chopped
2 roasted red (bell) peppers
6 hard-boiled/cooked eggs (see page 10), peeled
6 bay leaves
olive oil, to drizzle
sea salt and black pepper, to season
Potato Salad (see page 124), to serve

marinade
1 teaspoon each of dried thyme, oregano, marjoram and sea salt
½ teaspoon dried chilli/ hot red pepper flakes
2 garlic cloves, crushed
60 ml/¼ cup red wine vinegar
60 ml/¼ cup olive oil

serves 6–8

Rinse the steak under cold water and pat dry with paper towels. Put the meat between two pieces of clingfilm/plastic wrap and, using a mallet, pound the meat until it is paper thin, being careful not to tear it. Remove the clingfilm/ plastic wrap and place the steak in a ceramic dish. Mix together and pour over the marinade and refrigerate for 6–24 hours.

Preheat the oven to 190°C (375°F) Gas 5. Remove the steak from the fridge and lay out on a large piece of clingfilm/plastic wrap.

Finely julienne the chard and put in a mixing bowl. Add the Parmesan cheese, garlic, olives, parsley, marjoram and oregano and mix together. Season with salt and pepper to taste.

Spread the chard mixture evenly over the steak until you have completely covered it, then layer the peppers on top. Lay the boiled/cooked eggs in a row down the centre of the steak.

Taking the side of the steak nearest to you, roll up the meat like a cigar. Tie securely with kitchen twine at even intervals along the steak, making sure you tuck the end in. Lay in a roasting pan and slip the bay leaves under the twine. Season generously, with salt and pepper, then drizzle with olive oil.

Cook in the preheated oven for 1 hour, then remove from the oven. Cover loosely with foil and allow to rest for 20 minutes.

Cut thick slices and serve hot with a potato salad.

This Thai-inspired salad makes use of a rich peanut dressing to contrast with the fresh vegetables and creamy hard-boiled/cooked eggs.

salad kaek (pictured)

peanut (or sunflower) oil, for deep-frying
2 blocks of firm tofu/beancurd, about 5-cm/2-inches square
125 g/2 cups beansprouts, rinsed, drained and trimmed
125 g/2 cups Chinese long beans, chopped into 2.5-cm/1-inch lengths
2 medium tomatoes, thinly sliced
½ cucumber, thinly sliced
¼ white cabbage, thinly sliced, then broken into strands

2 hard-boiled/cooked eggs (see page 10), peeled and quartered

peanut dressing
2 tablespoons peanut (or sunflower) oil
1 tablespoon red curry paste
300 ml/1¼ cups coconut milk
½ teaspoon sea salt
1 tablespoon caster/granulated sugar
4 tablespoons crushed peanuts

serves 4

To make the peanut dressing, heat the oil in a wok or frying pan/skillet and stir in the curry paste. Add the coconut milk and stir well. Add the salt, sugar and peanuts and stir well. Cook briefly until the coconut milk comes to a boil, then remove immediately from the heat.

To make the salad, fill a wok or saucepan about one-third full with the peanut oil and heat until a scrap of noodle fluffs up immediately. Using a slotted spoon, add the tofu/beancurd to the hot oil and deep-fry until golden. Remove with a slotted spoon, drain on paper towels and set aside.

Arrange all the vegetables and eggs in a salad bowl. Thinly slice the tofu/beancurd and put the slices in the bowl. Serve with the peanut dressing.

Serve this sumptuous potato salad on its own, alongside the Matambre on page 123 for a delicious meal or with the Pâté de Campagne on page 95 for a satisfying picnic lunch.

potato salad

575 g/1¼ lbs. baby new potatoes, cleaned and halved if large
a small bunch of fresh parsley, chopped
3 spring onions/scallions, thinly sliced
2 teaspoons capers
2 soft-boiled/cooked eggs (see page 10), peeled and quartered
2 tablespoons mayonnaise (see right)
black pepper, to season

serves 4

mayonnaise (optional)
3 egg yolks
2 teaspoons white wine vinegar
1 teaspoon Dijon mustard
300 ml/1¼ cups olive oil
sea salt and black pepper, to season

makes 300 ml/1¼ cups

Fill a large saucepan with cold water, add the potatoes and bring to a boil. Reduce the heat and simmer until tender. Drain, then cool the potatoes under cold running water.

Put the parsley, spring onions/scallions and capers in a mixing bowl. Add the cold potatoes, stir in the mayonnaise, season with black pepper and mix well. Festoon with the egg quarters and serve.

mayonnaise
Put the egg yolks, vinegar and mustard in a bowl. Season lightly. Blend until frothy using an electric handheld whisk. With the motor running, drizzle in the olive oil and continue blending until the sauce is thick and glossy. Store in the fridge for up to 3 days.

Ham and peas are a classic combination and this simple dish is a perfect illustration of 'umami synergy' where the sweetness of the onions and peas combine with the salty pancetta and smooth, soft yolk of an egg.

peas, ham & eggs (pictured)

a good glug of olive oil
100 g/3½ oz. cubed
  pancetta or bacon
1 onion, thinly sliced
1 garlic clove, thinly sliced
425 g/15 oz. frozen or
  canned peas
100 ml/7 tablespoons
  chicken stock
a sprig of fresh mint,
  leaves only
4 large eggs
sea salt and black pepper,
  to season
pea shoots, to garnish

serves 1

Heat the olive oil in a large frying pan/skillet over medium heat and sauté the pancetta or bacon.

When cooked through, add the onion slices and garlic. Sauté until the onion begins to colour and the pancetta or bacon begins to crisp up.

Add the peas to the pan with the stock and the mint leaves, season with a little black pepper and leave to cook over low heat with the lid on until most of the stock has evaporated. Set aside.

Fill a medium saucepan with water and bring to a boil. Add the eggs and time for 6–7 minutes, as you want them gooey in the middle. Remove the eggs with a slotted spoon and refresh in cold water to stop them from cooking.

Peel the eggs and slice them in half lengthways. Season with a sprinkling of salt and pepper and lay on top of the warm peas.

Garnish the plate with pea shoots and serve immediately.

Pickled eggs are such a great accompaniment to salads. Halve them, sprinkle with black pepper and serve on a summer spread.

Szechuan pickled eggs

12 eggs
2 teaspoons Szechuan
  seasoning
4–6 bay leaves
235 ml/1 cup apple cider
  vinegar

a sterilized glass jar with an
  airtight lid

makes 12

Bring a large pan of water to a boil, add the eggs, and boil for 10 minutes. Remove the eggs from the boiling water with a slotted spoon and put in a large bowl filled with ice cubes and water to suspend the cooking process.

When the eggs are cold to the touch, peel and arrange in a large sterilized glass jar. Add the Szechuan seasoning and bay leaves and pour over the apple cider vinegar. Screw the lid on tighhtly and store in the fridge for at least 1 month before serving.

Once opened, keep refrigerated and consume within 3 months.

cook's note

Swap the Szechuan seasoning for any strong-flavoured herb or spice. Saffron threads work very well and colour the eggs in a light golden hue. Chipotle chilli/chile flakes also give good flavour.

This is an unusual but traditional Moroccan recipe. When prepared in a tagine, the eggs are cooked in the dish with the meatballs, on top of the sauce. This recipe cooks the eggs separately, allowing for preparation in an ordinary straight-sided frying pan/skillet. If you feel the need to include something green, add some frozen peas with the meatballs. This addition is not authentic, but is very tasty. Serve with bread to mop up the aromatic tomato sauce.

meatball tagine

½ onion, roughly chopped
a few sprigs of fresh
  parsley
a few sprigs of fresh
  coriander/cilantro
500 g/1 lb. 2 oz. ground
  lamb
1½ teaspoons sea salt
½ teaspoon ground white
  pepper
1 teaspoon ground cumin
1 teaspoon paprika
1 tablespoon fresh
  breadcrumbs
4 eggs, to serve

tomato sauce
1½ onions, roughly
  chopped
a small handful of fresh
  parsley
2 garlic cloves
400 g/2 cups canned
  chopped tomatoes
300 ml/1¼ cups stock
  (chicken, lamb or
  vegetable)
1½ teaspoons ground
  cumin
1 teaspoon ground white
  pepper
¼ teaspoon ground
  cinnamon
cayenne pepper, to taste
a pinch of caster/
  granulated sugar

serves 4

128 main meals

To make the meatballs, put the onion in a food processor with the parsley and coriander/cilantro. Process until finely chopped. Add the lamb and process, using the pulse button, to obtain a smooth paste. Transfer to a large mixing bowl.

Add the salt, pepper, cumin, paprika and breadcrumbs. Mix well with your hands to combine. Form into walnut-sized balls and transfer to a baking sheet. Cover and set aside.

To make the sauce, put the onions, parsley and garlic in a food processor and process until finely chopped. Transfer to a shallow frying pan/skillet large enough to hold the meatballs in a single layer. Add the tomatoes,

stock, cumin, pepper, cinnamon, ¼–½ teaspoon of cayenne pepper, depending on personal taste, and sugar. Stir and bring to a boil, then lower the heat and simmer, covered, for 15 minutes.

Nestle the meatballs in the sauce in a single layer. Cover and simmer for 20–30 minutes, until cooked through.

To serve, divide the meatballs and sauce between shallow soup plates or large bowls, arranging the meatballs in a ring around the perimeter. Poach or lightly fry the eggs (see pages 10–11), keeping the yolks runny, and place one cooked egg in the middle of each bowl. Serve immediately.

This is something like a freshly baked pide (Turkish bread) opened up like a pizza and called a pie. The dough is often filled or topped with the freshest of vegetables, such as tomatoes, spinach or chard, or tangy feta cheese and with an egg or two cracked on top before being baked. It doesn't matter if the yolk is a bit hard once baked – the combination of flavours will be heavenly all the same.

Swiss chard, feta & egg pie

3 tablespoons olive oil
2 garlic cloves, sliced
1 red onion, sliced
500 g/1 lb. 2 oz. Swiss chard, cut into 2-cm/¾-inch pieces
4 eggs
200 g/1½ cups feta cheese, crumbled
sea salt and black pepper, to season

dough

250 g/2 cups plain/all-purpose flour
150 g/1 stick plus 2 tablespoons butter, cubed
2 egg yolks
2–3 tablespoons iced water

serves 6

To make the dough, put the flour and butter in the bowl of a food processor and put the bowl in the freezer for 10 minutes. Pulse the ingredients a few times until just combined. With the motor running, add the egg yolks and just enough iced water so that the mixture is on the verge of coming together. Do not overbeat, as this will make the dough tough. Remove from the bowl and use lightly floured hands to quickly form it into a ball. Wrap in clingfilm/plastic wrap and let rest in the fridge for 30 minutes.

Put 2 tablespoons of the oil in a frying pan/skillet set over high heat, add the onion and garlic and cook for 2 minutes, until it softens and just flavours the oil. Add the Swiss chard to the pan and cook for about 5 minutes, stirring often, until it wilts and softens. Season well with salt and pepper, leave in the pan and set aside to cool.

Preheat the oven to 220°C (425°F) Gas 7. Roll the dough out on a sheet of lightly floured baking parchment to form a circle about 35 cm/14 inches in diameter, trimming away any uneven bits. Roll the edge over to form a 1-cm/⅜-inch border, then roll over again. Transfer the pastry circle to a baking sheet. Spoon the Swiss chard mixture over the dough.

Put the eggs in a bowl and prick the yolks with a fork. Pour the eggs over the Swiss chard so that they are evenly distributed, then scatter the feta cheese over the top. Drizzle the remaining oil over the pie and cook in the preheated oven for about 20 minutes, until the dough is golden and the top of the pie is just starting to turn brown.

Let cool for 10 minutes before cutting into slices to serve.

When the Italian asparagus season is in full flush, it is celebrated with great gusto. Asparagus of all types is for sale, the most prized being the fat white asparagus. It is usually cooked beyond al dente to bring out the flavour. A poached egg with its river of yellow yolk adds to the creaminess of this risotto and gives a wonderful contrast of textures.

asparagus risotto with a poached egg & Parmesan cheese

500 g/1 lb. 2 oz. fresh green or purple-tipped asparagus

about 1.5 litres/quarts hot vegetable (or light chicken) stock

1 teaspoon tarragon wine vinegar (or white wine vinegar)

6 eggs, cracked into individual cups

125 g/1 stick plus ½ tablespoon butter

2 large shallots, finely chopped

500 g/2½ cups risotto rice, preferably carnaroli

50 g/⅔ cup freshly grated Parmesan cheese

sea salt and black pepper, to season

to serve

1 tablespoon chopped fresh parsley and tarragon, mixed

Parmesan shavings

serves 6

Trim the base from each asparagus stem, but do no more than that. Put the stock in a wide saucepan and heat to simmering. Add the asparagus and boil for about 6 minutes until just tender. Drain, reserving the asparagus-flavoured stock and transferring it to another saucepan to simmer. Plunge the asparagus into a bowl of cold water to cool and set the colour, then cut into small pieces. If the ends of the asparagus stalks are very tough, cut them off, halve them and scrape out the insides and reserve. Add the tough parts to the stock.

To poach the eggs, fill a medium saucepan with cold water and bring to a boil. When the water is boiling, add the wine vinegar, then give it a good stir to create a whirlpool. Slip an egg into the vortex, then simmer very gently for 2–3 minutes. Using a slotted spoon, transfer the poached egg to a pan of warm water. Repeat the same procedure with the other eggs. Keep them warm while you make the risotto.

Melt half the butter in a large saucepan over medium heat and add the shallots. Cook gently for 5–6 minutes until soft, golden and translucent but not browned. Add the rice and asparagus scrapings to the shallots and stir until well coated with the butter and heated through. Begin adding the stock, a large ladle at a time (keeping back the asparagus trimmings), stirring gently until each ladle has almost been absorbed by the rice. The risotto should be kept at a bare simmer throughout cooking, so don't let the rice dry out – add more stock as necessary. Continue until the rice is tender and creamy, but the grains still firm. (This should take 15–20 minutes depending on the type of rice used – check the packet instructions.)

Taste and season well with salt and pepper and beat in the remaining butter and all the Parmesan cheese. Fold in the drained asparagus. Cover, let rest for a few minutes so the risotto can relax and the asparagus heat through, then serve immediately. You may like to add a little more hot stock to the risotto just before you serve to loosen it, but don't let it wait around too long or the rice will turn mushy. Serve the risotto topped with a drained poached egg, sprinkled with parsley, tarragon and Parmesan shavings.

Sometimes called 'mee krob', this crispy noodle dish is is an indulgent treat. Be careful when deep-frying noodles and be amazed as the beaten egg transforms into a lacy cake as the oil bubbles up quite dramatically.

mee grob

100 g/3½ oz. dried rice vermicelli noodles
vegetable oil, for deep-frying
2 eggs, beaten
125 g/1 cup firm tofu/beancurd, cubed
1 tablespoon dried shrimp
1 Asian shallot, thinly sliced
1 tablespoon pickled garlic
50 g/1 cup beansprouts, trimmed
a small bunch of fresh coriander/cilantro
6 garlic chives, roughly chopped

sauce
125 g/½ cup plus 1 tablespoon grated palm sugar
1 tablespoon yellow bean paste
2 tablespoons fish sauce
1 tablespoon freshly squeezed lime juice

serves 4

Put the noodles in a bowl, cover with boiling water and soak for 20 minutes until softened. Drain the noodles and pat dry with paper towels.

Next make the sauce. Put the palm sugar in a saucepan with 1 tablespoon cold water set over low heat. Heat gently, stirring continuously, until the sugar dissolves. Turn up the heat and boil for a minute until the syrup turns lightly golden, then stir in the yellow bean paste, fish sauce and lime juice. Simmer gently for 3–4 minutes until thick and keep warm until ready to use.

Pour vegetable oil into a wok or large saucepan to reach about 5 cm/2 inches up the side and set over medium–high heat. Heat until a cube of bread dropped into the oil crisps in 30 seconds. Add the noodles in small bunches and fry for 1–2 minutes until crisp and golden. Remove with a slotted spoon and drain on paper towels. Repeat with the remaining noodles until you have fried them all. Keep the pan on the heat.

Break the noodles into a large mixing bowl and set aside.

Strain the beaten egg through a fine-mesh sieve/strainer and pour half into the hot oil – it will puff up into a lacy cake. Fry for 30 seconds, flip over and fry for a further 30 seconds until crisp and brown, then remove with a slotted spoon. Drain on paper towels and repeat with the remaining egg.

Deep-fry the tofu/beancurd and set aside.

Deep-fry the dried shrimp for 10 seconds, remove with a slotted spoon and set aside.

Carefully discard all but 1 tablespoon of the oil and stir-fry the shallot and garlic for 5 minutes until lightly crisp. Stir in the beansprouts and remove the pan from the heat.

Add all the fried ingredients along with the coriander/cilantro and garlic chives to the noodles and stir to combine. Pour in the sauce, stir again and serve at once.

Ramen is a Japanese noodle dish where the noodles are drenched in meat or fish broth and topped with pork belly, dried seaweed, spring onions/scallions and, finally, lightly flavoured boiled/cooked eggs.

shio ramen

1 tablespoon sake
1 tablespoon mirin
1 garlic clove, crushed
1 teaspoon freshly grated ginger
50 ml/¼ cup dark soy sauce
50 ml/¼ cup light soy sauce
1 tablespoon caster/granulated sugar
a 750-g/1½-lb. piece of pork belly
4 eggs
2 litres/quarts chicken stock
250 g/9 oz. dried ramen noodles
spring onions/scallions, thinly sliced to garnish

serves †

Pour the sake and mirin into a small saucepan set over medium heat and bring slowly to a boil. Add the garlic, ginger, dark and light soy sauces and the sugar, and stir until the sugar dissolves. Bring to a boil and simmer very gently for 5 minutes. Remove from the heat and leave to cool.

Cut the pork belly in half across the grain to make two similar squares and put in a saucepan into which the pork fits snugly.

Pour over the cooled soy mixture, return to the heat and bring to a boil. Cover and simmer gently for 1 hour or until the pork is tender. Remove the pan from the heat but leave the pork in the stock to cool at room temperature. Remove the pork from the stock, reserving the stock, and cut into thick slices. Set aside.

Put the eggs in a saucepan of cold water and set over high heat. Bring to a boil and simmer for 5 minutes. Remove the eggs from the pan and immediately rinse under cold running water until they are cool enough to handle. Peel the eggs and place them in a clean bowl. Pour over the reserved stock and leave to soak for 30 minutes. Lift the eggs from the stock and cut in half lengthways.

Meanwhile bring the chicken stock to a boil in a large saucepan and simmer until reduced by about one-third to 1.25 litres/quarts. Remove from the heat and stir in 4 tablespoons of the reserved pork stock. Add the pork belly slices and warm through for 5 minutes.

Plunge the noodles into a saucepan of boiling water, return to a boil and cook for about 4 minutes or until al dente. Drain well, then divide the noodles between soup bowls. Spoon over the stock and pork slices, add two egg halves to each bowl and serve garnished with the spring onions/scallions.

Asian or 'nashi' pears are commonly added to Korean sauces but are also delicious when grated into salads. Serve in summer months when the combination of chilled ingredients with tangy sauce is refreshingly tasty.

chilled noodles with egg

250 g/9 oz. dried soba noodles
2 eggs
1 carrot, peeled and trimmed
1 small cucumber, peeled and deseeded
1 Asian pear, peeled and thinly sliced
100 g/1¾ cups beansprouts
a handful each of mizuna leaves and perilla leaves (optional)
a pinch of sesame seeds, toasted, to serve
Spicy Kimchi (see page 66) or store-bought, to serve

cho-gochujang
1 tablespoon sesame seeds
1–2 teaspoons gochujang
2 tablespoons rice wine vinegar
2 tablespoons dark soy sauce
1 tablespoon clear honey
2 teaspoons sesame oil
1 spring onion/scallion, trimmed and finely chopped
1 garlic clove, crushed

serves 1

Cook the noodles by plunging them into a large saucepan of boiling water. Return to a boil and cook for 4 minutes until al dente. Drain and immediately refresh under cold water before draining again. Shake to remove any excess water and set aside.

Put the eggs in a saucepan of cold water and set over high heat. Bring to a boil and simmer for 8 minutes. Remove the eggs from the pan and immediately rinse under cold, running water until they are cool enough to handle. Peel the eggs and place them in a bowl.

Cut the carrot and cucumber into thin strips and put in a large mixing bowl.

Add the noodles to the bowl and toss with the pear, beansprouts, and mizuna and perilla leaves, if using.

To make the cho-gochujang, Dry-fry the sesame seeds in a small frying pan/skillet set over medium heat until evenly toasted. Transfer to a spice grinder or pestle and mortar and grind to a rough paste. Put the ground sesame seeds in a small bowl and stir in the gochujang, vinegar, soy sauce, honey and sesame oil until smooth, then add the spring onion/scallion and garlic and stir well. Serve immediately.

Divide the noodle mixture between serving dishes.

Cut the eggs in half and place one half on each salad. Drizzle over a little of the cho-gochujang and sprinkle with the sesame seeds. Serve with kimchi.

cook's note
Native to the mountainous regions of Asia, perilla is a member of the mint family but is sometimes referred to as 'sesame leaves' (though unrelated). They appear similar to nettle leaves and can be substituted with mint or Thai basil if unavailable.

desserts & drinks

Soufflés are one of the most iconic French desserts and they can take a long time to master. However, this simple lemon mousse made in a ramekin and shaped with the help of some baking parchment and an elastic band looks like a soufflé without any of the fuss. The recipe works just as well with oranges and grapefruit, too.

chilled lemon soufflés

4 leaves of gelatine
6 eggs, separated
500 ml/2 cups whipping
  cream
300 g/1½ cups caster/
  superfine sugar
grated zest and juice of
  4 lemons, plus extra
  zest to decorate
icing/confectioners'
  sugar, to dust

variation (optional)
8–12 fresh raspberries (or
  8 amarena cherries)

4 ramekins

makes 4

Start the recipe the day before you want to serve the soufflés.

First prepare the ramekins. Measure their circumference and add 1 cm/½ inch to the figure. Now measure their height and add 5 cm/2 inches to the figure. Take some baking parchment and draw four rectangles: their length should match that of the recorded circumference; and their height should match that of the recorded height. Cut out the rectangles of parchment and wrap each one around a ramekin. Fasten tightly in place with an elastic band or some sticky tape. Place on a baking sheet and set aside.

Put the gelatine in a bowl of cold water to soften.

Put the egg whites in a stand mixer or in a bowl using an electric handheld whisk and whisk until firm peaks form. Refrigerate while you continue with the recipe.

Put the cream in the stand mixer or in a bowl using an electric handheld whisk again and whisk until soft peaks form. Don't over-beat otherwise it will go stiff and grainy and look split.

Put the egg yolks and sugar in a heatproof bowl over a pan of simmering water (not letting the base of the bowl touch the water). Whisk with a balloon whisk for 5 minutes or until light and foamy. This is called a 'sabayon'.

Put the lemon zest and juice in a saucepan over medium heat and bring to a boil. Remove from the heat and stir in the softened gelatine, squeezed of excess water.

Add the lemon mixture to the sabayon, whisking quickly until thoroughly combined.

Gently fold the egg whites into the lemon sabayon with a large, metal spoon. When evenly incorporated, fold in the whipped cream in the same way.

Divide the mixture between the ramekins with a spoon – it should reach above the rim of the ramekins by about 3 cm/1¼ inches and be contained by the parchment to give you that restaurant 'soufflé' look.

Allow to set in the fridge overnight.

The next day, dust with icing/confectioners' sugar and a little extra lemon zest to serve.

variation
For a hidden little treat, add 2–3 fresh raspberries or amarena cherries to the base of each ramekin before you spoon in the mixture.

Everyone adores the silky baked egg custard that is crème caramel.
Sometimes served in individual moulds, this dish is served whole,
as it is in Spain, where it is known as 'flan casero'.

crème caramel (pictured)

450 g/2¼ cups caster/
granulated sugar
1 litre/quart whole milk
2 teaspoons vanilla
extract
10 eggs

serves 10–12

Put half of the sugar in an ovenproof frying pan/skillet and set over medium heat. Cook until it is just golden around the sides of the pan. Increase the heat and gently swirl the pan so the sugar dissolves and turns the colour of honey. Remove from the heat and continue swirling the pan until the caramel starts to set on the sides.

Preheat the oven to 180°C (350°F) Gas 4 and put the pan with the caramel inside a large roasting pan.

Heat the milk and vanilla extract together in a saucepan set over medium heat until just boiling. Put the eggs and remaining sugar in a bowl and whisk until well combined. Add the hot milk to the egg mixture and whisk to combine.

Strain through a fine-mesh sieve/strainer, then pour the custard into the pan with the caramel. Pour enough cold water into the roasting pan to surround the pan with the custard in it and transfer to the preheated oven.

Cook for 1¼ hours, until the custard has set. It may still be slightly wobbly in the centre.

Carefully lift the pan with the custard out of the roasting pan and cool at room temperature. Refrigerate for at least 3 hours or ideally overnight.

Run a knife around the side of the pan, sit a serving plate larger than the pan over the top and quickly turn the flan out onto the plate. Tap the bottom of the pan to release the flan and serve.

To finish off a great pie or crumble, all you need is a dollop of pouring custard, also known as 'crème anglaise'.

crème anglaise

600 ml/2½ cups whole
milk
1 vanilla pod/bean, split
6 egg yolks
2 tablespoons caster/
granulated sugar

serves 8–10

Put the milk and vanilla in a saucepan and set over very low heat until it reaches boiling point. Remove from the heat and set aside for 20 minutes, after which you can discard the vanilla.

Whisk the egg yolks and sugar together in a bowl until pale and creamy, then stir in the vanilla-infused milk. Return the mixture to the pan

and warm over medium heat, stirring constantly with a wooden spoon. Do not let the sauce boil. When the mixture has thickened so that it coats the back of the spoon, remove from the heat.

Serve hot, or if you prefer to serve it cold, cover the surface with clingfilm/plastic wrap to prevent a skin forming, and leave to cool.

Nothing says summer quite like pavlova. Egg whites become crisp meringue with a soft marshmallowy centre, paired with fresh berries, whipped cream and a tangy passion fruit curd.

pavlova with fresh strawberries & passion fruit curd

6 egg whites
a pinch of salt
375 g/2 cups caster/
   superfine sugar
3 teaspoons cornflour/
   cornstarch
1½ teaspoons white wine
   vinegar
½ teaspoon vanilla
   extract

passion fruit curd
4 passion fruit
1 large egg, plus 2 large
   egg yolks
75 g/5 tablespoons butter
115 g/½ cup plus 1
   tablespoon caster/
   granulated sugar
1 teaspoon freshly
   squeezed lime juice

topping
500 ml/2 cups whipping/
   heavy cream
5 passion fruit
300 g/3 cups fresh
   strawberries, hulled and
   halved

serves 6–8

Begin by making the passion fruit curd. Place the pulp and seeds of the passion fruit in a food processor and blitz to loosen the seeds. Strain into a jug/pitcher through a fine-mesh sieve/strainer. Put the egg and egg yolks in a mixing bowl and whisk to combine. Set aside. Put the butter with the sugar and strained passion fruit juice in a small saucepan set over low heat, and stir until the butter has melted and the sugar has dissolved.

Pour one-third of the butter mixture into the whisked eggs, then return to the pan.

Continue to cook gently, stirring continuously with a wooden spoon, until the mixture has thickened and coats the back of the spoon. It is important not to let the mixture get too hot as it will scramble the eggs and may curdle.

Remove from the heat and stir through the lime juice and the pulp of the remaining passion fruit.

Press a piece of clingfilm/plastic wrap onto the surface of the curd to prevent a skin forming and set in the fridge for 1 hour, or until chilled.

Preheat the oven to 180°C (350°F) Gas 4. Draw a 25-cm/10-inch

diameter circle onto a piece of baking parchment, then turn the paper over and place on a baking sheet.

In a clean, dry bowl, whisk the egg whites and salt to soft peaks. Add the sugar, one-third at a time, whisking after each addition until the peaks become stiff and shiny. Sprinkle the cornflour/cornstarch, vinegar and vanilla over the whisked whites, and gently fold until just combined.

Heap the meringue onto the baking parchment within the marked circle and use a large spoon or spatula to flatten the top and shape into a circle.

Put in the preheated oven and immediately reduce the heat to 150°C (300°F) Gas 2. Cook for 1¼ hours, then turn off the oven, open the door and leave the meringue to cool completely in the oven.

For the topping, whisk the cream until just whipped, then fold through half of the chilled passion fruit curd.

Turn the pavlova over onto a plate and peel off the baking parchment. Turn back over, then spoon the passion fruit cream onto the meringue base. Layer with more passion fruit curd and top with fresh passion fruit pulp and strawberries.

The lemon tart is a French classic that is commonly found on restaurant dessert menus around the world. Sweet and tangy filling encased in a rich pâté sucrée (sweet shortcrust pastry) case makes for the perfect palate-cleansing after-dinner treat.

tarte au citron

100 g/7 tablespoons
  butter, softened
100 g/1 cup caster/
  granulated sugar
1 vanilla bean/pod
finely grated zest of
  1 lemon
2 eggs, lightly beaten
250 g/2 cups plain/
  all-purpose flour
icing/confectioners'
  sugar, to dust

filling
9 eggs
400 g/2 cups caster/
  granulated sugar
juice and grated zest
  of 5 lemons
275 ml/1 cup plus
  2 tablespoons double/
  heavy cream

a 20-cm/8-in. tart pan,
  greased and lightly
  dusted with flour
baking beans

serves 6–8

To make the pâté sucrée, beat the butter and sugar together in a stand mixer or in a bowl with an electric handheld whisk until pale – about 5 minutes. Split the vanilla pod/bean lengthways using a small, sharp knife and scrape the seeds out into the creamed butter mixture. Add the lemon zest and beat again to incorporate. With the whisk running, gradually add the eggs, mixing until fully incorporated. Gently mix in the flour but do not over-work the dough, otherwise the gluten will develop and you will end up with pastry that is tough rather than crisp and light. Bring the dough together into a ball with your hands, wrap in clingfilm/plastic wrap and refrigerate for at least 2 hours, but overnight if possible.

Preheat the oven to 180°C (350°F) Gas 4.

Take the pâté sucrée out of the fridge and roll out on a lightly floured surface to a rough circle at about 25 cm/10 inches in diameter.

Loosely wrap the pastry around the rolling pin and transfer it to the prepared tart pan. Unravel the pastry into the pan. Gently coax the pastry neatly into the curves and angles of the pan, press lightly into the sides and cut off any excess with a small, sharp knife.

Lay a sheet of baking parchment over the pan and fill with baking beans. Put on a baking sheet and bake in the preheated oven for 10–15 minutes.

Lower the oven temperature to 160°C (325°F) Gas 3. Remove the paper and beans from the tart pan and return the tart case to the oven for 5–10 minutes. Remove from the oven.

Lower the temperature to 130°C (250°F) Gas ½.

For the filling, put the eggs and sugar in a mixing bowl and whisk with a balloon whisk just to combine. Whisk in the lemon juice and zest. Finally, stir in the cream. Pour the mixture into a jug/pitcher.

Put the tart case back into the oven, as far forward as you can without the pan falling off the oven shelf. Pour the filling slowly into the tart case.

Push the tart further into the oven, close the door and bake for 30–40 minutes or until it just starts to set in the centre but still wobbles like a jelly. It will continue to cook when it is taken out of the oven, so don't be tempted to keep baking until it is fully set because it will curdle and split. Allow to cool completely, then remove from the pan.

Serve the tart whole or in slices, dusted with icing/confectioners' sugar, at room temperature.

The really great thing about making a semifreddo is that you don't need an ice cream maker. It freezes wonderfully in any container and you can serve it either in scoops or turned out onto a serving plate and sliced. The trick with making both ice cream and semifreddo is to warm the eggs very slowly like you would with custard (see Crème Anglaise, page 145). Take care not to let it scramble, and be sure to cool it very quickly.

tutti frutti semifreddo

3 eggs, plus 2 egg yolks
100 g/½ cup caster/
   granulated sugar
500 ml/2 cups double/
   heavy cream
3 tablespoons candied
   citrus fruit, finely
   chopped
cookies, to serve

serves 6–8

Combine the eggs, plus the yolks, and sugar in a heatproof bowl and set over a saucepan of simmering water. Whisk the mixture with an electric handheld whisk on high speed for about 5 minutes, until it turns into pale yellow ribbons and has thickened. Turn off the heat and place the bowl with the egg mixture over a bowl filled with iced water to cool.

Pour the cream into a large bowl and beat until thick and soft peaks form. Fold the cooled egg mixture through the cream until thoroughly incorporated. Fold in the candied citrus fruit and pour into a clean bowl. Cover with clingfilm/plastic wrap and freeze until firm.

Scoop and serve with cookies.

cook's note

You can also line a loaf pan with clingfilm/plastic wrap and pour in the semifreddo. Once frozen invert the pan onto a serving plate and unmold. Cut into 4-cm/1½-inch slices to serve.

Egg white cocktails aren't for everyone but the whipped white can add to the flavour of a drink. Flavour is made up of not just taste and aroma, but also mouthfeel and appearance. That light frothy cloud that sits on the cocktail's surface not only makes the drink look fantastic but will lend it a fluffy lightness that helps it slip down smoothly.

commodore cocktail (pictured)

50 ml/2 oz. light Puerto
   Rican-style rum
25 ml/1 oz. fresh lemon
   juice
10 ml/2 barspoons
   grenadine
10 ml/2 barspoons
   raspberry syrup
5 ml/1 barspoon caster/
   superfine sugar
1 egg white

serves 1

Add all the ingredients to a cocktail shaker filled with ice and shake sharply to blend and whip up the egg white.

Strain into a frosted coupette glass and serve immediately while the froth is still at its best.

gin fizz

50 ml/2 oz. gin
25 ml/1 oz. lemon juice
   (or lime juice)
15 ml/1 tablespoon sugar
   syrup
1 egg white
soda water, to top up

serves 1

Add all the ingredients, except the soda, to a cocktail shaker filled with ice. Shake sharply for as long as you can (up to 5 minutes) to whip up the egg white.

Strain into a chilled Champagne flute, add a dash of soda water and serve immediately while the froth is still at its best.

In essence, eggnog is a mixture of cream (or milk), sugar, and beaten egg that can have alcohol added to it. Of the many variations around, this Baltimore eggnog uses three different types of alcohol and a dusting of spice to really add extra depth.

eggnog (pictured)

25 ml/1 oz. Madeira wine
12.5 ml/½ oz. Cognac
12.5 ml/½ oz. Jamaican rum
a pinch of ground cinnamon
1 tablespoon caster/ superfine sugar
1 egg
25 ml/1 oz. double/heavy cream
grated nutmeg, to serve

serves 1

Add all the ingredients except the nutmeg to a cocktail shaker and shake vigorously for 15 seconds.

Pour into glasses and grate over a little nutmeg, to serve.

This warming, festive drink with a hint of coffee makes a lovely alternative to the more traditional eggnog. For a non-alcoholic version, simply omit the rum.

eggnog latte

500 ml/2 cups whole milk
1 vanilla pod/bean, split
2 eggs
2–3 tablespoons caster/ granulated sugar, to taste
½ teaspoon ground cinnamon
a pinch of grated nutmeg
2 tablespoons dark rum
250 ml/1 cup freshly brewed hot coffee

serves 1

Put the milk and vanilla in a saucepan and heat gently until the milk just reaches boiling point.

Meanwhile, put the eggs, sugar and spices in a bowl and whisk until frothy. Stir in the milk, then return the mixture to the pan.

Heat gently for 2–3 minutes, stirring constantly with a wooden spoon, until the mixture thickens slightly.

Remove from the heat and stir in the rum and coffee. Pour into heatproof glasses and serve immediately.

A whipped-up egg or egg white cuts through the tart taste of these three 'sours'. Strictly speaking, a sour, as its name suggests, should err on the tart side, but these three versions offer varying degrees of tartness, from the tangy whiskey sour to the silky sweet krupnik sour.

whiskey sour (pictured)

1 egg white
freshly squeezed juice of
    1 lemon
12.5ml/½ oz. sugar syrup
50 ml/2 oz. bourbon
    whiskey
a few drops Angostura
    bitters (optional)
lemon zest, to garnish

serves 1

Ease the spring off the strainer and place it in the shaker with the egg white to whisk the white more effectively while the cocktail is being shaken.

Add the remaining ingredients and shake vigorously.

Pour into a glass filled with ice cubes. Garnish with the lemon zest.

krupnik sour

50 ml/2 oz. Krupnik vodka
50 ml/2 oz. fresh lemon
    juice
25 ml/1 oz. sugar syrup
1 large egg white
2 dashes of Angostura
    bitters
lemon slice, to garnish
maraschino cherry, to
    garnish

serves 1

Add all the ingredients to a shaker filled with ice. Shake the mixture and pour into an old-fashioned glass.

Garnish with a lemon slice and a maraschino cherry.

pisco sour

50 ml/2 oz. pisco
25 ml/1 oz. lemon juice
15 ml/1 tablespoon sugar
    syrup
1 egg white
2 dashes Angostura
    bitters

serves 1

Add all the ingredients to a shaker filled with ice. Shake sharply and strain into a Champagne flute.

index

credits

recipe credits

Valerie Aikman-Smith
Matambre; Spicy kimchi hash browns with poached eggs; Szechuan pickled eggs; Tutti frutti semifreddo

Miranda Ballard
Chorizo, avocado & poached egg open sandwich; The big breakfast burger with Portobello mushroom & fried egg; Roast ham omelette ; Scrambled egg, roast tomatoes & prosciutto with mushroom purée; Fried egg, tomato bread, jamón & fries; Pâté de campagne; Spaghetti carbonara

Ghillie Başan
Courgette/zucchini, feta & herb patties

Fiona Beckett
Goat's cheese omelette with wild garlic/ramps & chervil

Vatcharin Bhumichitr
Salad kaek

Jordan Bourke
Bibimbap

Maxine Clark
Artichoke & pecorino omelette; Fresh egg pasta; Quiche Lorraine; Asparagus risotto with a poached egg & Parmesan cheese

Linda Collister
Mini vegetable frittatas

Ross Dobson
Swiss chard, feta & egg pie; Crème caramel

Tori Finch
French dressing; Scotch quail eggs; Salade Niçoise with roast vine tomatoes

Ben Fordham & Felipe Fuentes Cruz
Huevos con chorizo

Tonia George
Scrambled eggs with smoked trout & shiso; Eggs Benedict; English breakfast quiche; Steak & fried egg baps with

mustard butter; Poached eggs on spinach with yogurt & spiced butter; Caramelized chicory with Black Forest ham & poached eggs; Smoked haddock, radish & avocado omelette wraps; Blinis with salmon & crème fraîche

Tori Haschka
Moroccan baked eggs; Bulgogi salad; Pea, basil & feta fritters with roast tomatoes

Carol Hilker
Steak & egg brunch skillet

Rachael Anne Hill
Scrambled eggs with smoked salmon; Kedgeree; Florentine baked eggs

Jennifer Joyce
Corned beef hash

Jenny Linford
Tunisian baked eggs in tomato sauce; Sun-dried tomato & rosemary cornbread; Menemen; Spinach & tomato soufflé

Claire & Lucy McDonald
Baked eggs with smoked mackerel; Potato salad

Jane Mason
Bread biscuits with a soft-boiled/cooked eggs

Dan May
Baked chilli/chile eggs; Huevos rancheros; Spanish omelette

Hannah Miles
Gluten-free English muffins; Cinnamon French toast; Cheese & onion soufflé muffins; Mini choc-chip pancakes; Pancake stack with whipped maple butter

Miisa Mink
Egg-rice pockets

Louise Pickford
Chilled noodles with egg; Mayonnaise; Mee grob; Shio ramen; Crème anglaise; Eggnog latte

Isidora Popovic
Roast potato & spring onion/scallion tartlets

Ben Reed
Commodore cocktail; Gin fizz; Eggnog; Pisco sour; Krupnik sour

Shelagh Ryan
Baked eggs with chorizo, mushrooms & lemon crème fraîche; Bubble & squeak with pear & apple chutney; Corn fritters with roast tomatoes & smashed avocados; Chorizo frittata bites; Dukkha eggs; Pavlova with fresh strawberries & passion fruit curd; Smoked haddock fishcakes with poached eggs & dill mayo

Laura Santtini
Peas, ham & eggs; Steak tartare with mustard cheese toasts

Milli Taylor
Devilled eggs; 'Scotch eggs'

Will Torrent
Chilled lemon soufflés; Tarte au citron

Fran Warde
Eggs 'en cocotte'

Laura Washburn
Mushrooms & egg on toast with fried tomatoes; Ham & egg breakfast quesadilla; Breakfast burrito; Breakfast bread & butter pudding with dried apricots & cranberries; Meatball tagine; Portobello egg cups

William Yeoward
Whiskey sour

picture credits

Front and back cover photography by **Jonathan Gregson**

Spine photography **Kate Whitaker**

Endpaper photography by **William Reavell**

All illustrations by **Jenny Seddon**

Food photography by:

Caroline Arber Page 68

Jan Baldwin Page 93

Martin Brigdale Pages 117, 129

Peter Cassidy Pages 32, 36, 49, 60, 64, 97, 101, 105, 118, 125

Helen Cathcart Page 89

Addie Chinn Page 156

Georgia Glynn-Smith Pages 6, 90, 113

Jonathan Gregson Pages 14, 17, 53, 58, 73, 74, 77, 143, 148

Richard Jung Pages 35, 130

Erin Kunkel Pages 67, 122, 151

Sandra Lane Page 3

William Lingwood Pages 152, 155

Jason Lowe Page 133

Steve Painter Pages 18, 27, 31, 39, 40, 46, 63, 86, 94, 114

Con Poulos Pages 102, 126

William Reavell Pages 22, 23, 83, 121, 144, 150

Ian Wallace Pages 134-138

Kate Whitaker Pages 2, 24-25, 43, 45, 54, 65, 70-71, 81, 98, 110, 147

Isobel Wield Pages 5, 28, 50, 57, 78, 109

Clare Winfield Pages 21, 103